TYPING POWER DRILLS

THIRD EDITION

Alan C. Lloyd, Ph.D.
Director of Career Advancement
The Olsten Corporation
Westbury, New York

Fred E. Winger, Ed.D.
Former Professor of Office Administration
  and Business Education
Oregon State University
Corvallis, Oregon

Carole Hoffman Eide
Instructor, Business and Office Education
Renton Vocational Technical Institute
Renton, Washington

Robert Gryder, Ed.D.
Professor, Department of Administrative
  Services
College of Business Administration, Arizona
  State University
Tempe, Arizona

M. Andrea Holmes
Instructor, Business and Office Education
Renton Vocational Technical Institute
Renton, Washington

Gregg Division/McGraw-Hill Book Company
New York ▪ Atlanta ▪ Dallas ▪ St. Louis ▪ San Francisco
Auckland ▪ Bogotá ▪ Guatemala ▪ Hamburg ▪ Johannesburg
Lisbon ▪ London ▪ Madrid ▪ Mexico ▪ Montreal ▪ New Delhi
Panama ▪ Paris ▪ San Juan ▪ São Paulo ▪ Singapore
Sydney ▪ Tokyo ▪ Toronto

S0-AKD-071

Sponsoring Editor   Diana M. Johnson
Editing Supervisor   Gloria Lewis
Design Supervisor   Meri Shardin
Production Director   Frank Bellantoni

Cover/interior design: Delgado Design Associates
Illustrator: Laura Hatman

Library of Congress Cataloging in Publication Data

Main entry under title:

Typing power drills.

Includes index.
1. Typewriting—Problems, exercises, etc.   I. Lloyd, Alan C.
Z49.2.T96 1984   652.3'07   83-8592
ISBN 0-07-038176-3

Typing Power Drills, Third Edition

67890 KGPKGP 89876

ISBN 0-07-038176-3

WHAT YOU WILL FIND IN THIS BOOK

INDEX TO THE DRILLS IN THIS BOOK

The numbers shown here are drill numbers, not page numbers. The drill numbers are shown in the left margin and bottom left corner of each page. All-capital entries are actual names of the drills in this book.

HOW TO USE THIS BOOK

The third edition of *Typing Power Drills* incorporates a new feature—the Pretest/Practice/Posttest routine—to help you achieve your objective: to *correct, improve,* or *perfect* your typing techniques and habits. Based on the authors' research and on suggestions from teachers of many of the students who used the two very popular previous editions, this third edition contains practice drills designed to help you achieve your goal of typing power—greater speed and accuracy.

One way to reach your goal is to type straight through the book, typing every line repetitively. But a quicker, surer way is to use one of the two skill-building plans that this book offers:

1. *Selective Skill Development.* The list on the inside front cover allows you to select *your* specific typing problems and the corresponding drills that will help you correct those problems. By concentrating time and effort on those drills, you will overcome *your* individual problems.

2. *Complete Skill-Building Program.* Skill building benefits anyone who types by touch. It is a positive learning experience involving three major components: (a) proper position at the typewriter, (b) efficient manipulation of the keyboard, and (c) selective drill practice using the Pretest/Practice/Posttest routine (based on action research conducted by Dr. Fred E. Winger in 1972–1973). A complete skill-building program includes:

   a. *Diagnostic Pretest.* The *Pretest* helps you identify your stroking strengths and weaknesses.

   b. *Selective Practice.* Selective *Practice* gives you the opportunity to practice the drill material necessary to correct specific weaknesses and thereby develops increased skill. Results will be even quicker if you follow this direction: *If your basic need is greater accuracy,* type each set of drill lines as though it were a paragraph, repeating not individual lines but the whole "paragraph" as a unit. *But if your basic need is greater speed,* practice the material line by line (that is, repeat each line several times before starting the next).

   c. *Posttest.* The *Posttest* allows you to measure your achievement since you took the Pretest and thus provides you with immediate feedback on your skill development. The Pretest/Practice/Posttest routine allows you, and your teacher, to measure your progress, and it provides direction in the selection of additional drill materials.

Other new features of *Typing Power Drills, Third Edition,* include a drill section on common words found in written business communications (based on a 1981 study conducted by Dr. Scot Ober and funded by the Arizona Department of Education) and a drill section on computer vocabulary words.

Power typing—keyboarding skill—is becoming more important than ever before as a result of today's technology. It is the communication skill of tomorrow, and tomorrow is now!

The Authors

TECHNIQUE
REVIEW

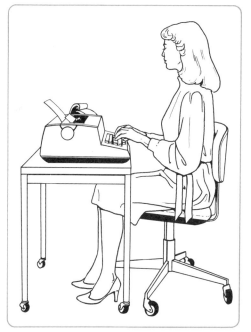

The proper position of hands, body, and feet at the typewriter plays a major role in the development of maximum speed and greater accuracy.

BODY POSITION

- Head erect and facing the copy.
- Back straight with body leaning slightly forward; shoulders level and parallel with your desk.
- Body a handspan from the machine, centered opposite the J key.

FEET

- Feet firmly on the floor in front of your chair.
- One foot a little ahead of the other, with 6 or 7 inches between your ankles.

HANDS

- Palms low but not touching the machine.
- Hands flat and level across their backs.
- Thumb above the center of space bar.
- Hands so close that you could lock thumbs.
- Fingers curved so that you can type on their tips. Fingernails cut short.

Take 1-minute timings on each paragraph before taking 3-minute timings on the entire page.

18   An ever-growing number of complex and rigid rules plus   12
hard-to-cope-with regulations are now being legislated from   24
state to state. Key federal regulations were formulated by   36
the FDA, FTC, and the CPSC. Each of these federal agencies   48
serves a specific mission. One example: Laws sponsored by   60
the Office of the Fair Debt Collection Practices prevent an   72
agency from purposefully harassing clients in serious debt.   84

19   The Fair Packaging and Labeling Act makes certain that   12   96
protection from misleading packaging of goods is guaranteed   24 108
to each buyer of goods carried in small shops as well as in   36 120
large supermarkets. Products on the market must reveal the   48 132
names of all ingredients on the label. Language must be in   60 144
clear and precise terms that can be understood by everyone.   72 156
This practice is very crucial for the lives of many people.   84 168

20   It is prudent that we recall that the FDA specifically   12 180
requires that all goods are pure, safe, and wholesome. The   24 192
FDA states that all goods be produced under highly sanitary   36 204
conditions. Drugs must be completely safe and must also be   48 216
effective for their stated purpose. This policy applies to   60 228
cosmetics that must be both safe and pure. Individuals are   72 240
often totally unappreciative of the FDA's great dedication.   84 252

| 1 | 2 | 3 | 4 | 5 | 6 | 7 | 8 | 9 | 10 | 11 | 12

DRILLS

These smooth patterns will help build fluency and continuity. Start each drill very slowly; when you recognize its sequence, speed up gradually until you reach a peak speed.

1 HOME ROW

1 a ; s l d k f j g h a ; s l d k f j g h a ; s l d k f j g h
2 g h f j d k s l a ; g h f j d k s l a ; g h f j d k s l a ;
3 aa ;; ss ll dd kk ff jj gg hh ff jj dd kk ss ll aa ;; ss ll
4 a;sldkfjghfjdksla; a;sldkfjghfjdksla; a;sldkfjghfjdksla; a;
5 asdfg ;lkjh gfdsa hjkl; asdfg ;lkjh gfdsa hjkl; asdfg ;lkjh

2 HOME AND THIRD ROW

6 a q a q aq aq aqa aqa ; p ; p ;p ;p ;p; ;p; aqa ;p; aqa ;p;
7 s w s w sw sw sws sws l o l o lo lo lol lol sws lol sws lol
8 d e d e de de ded ded k i k i ki ki kik kik ded kik ded kik
9 f r f r fr fr frf frf j u j u ju ju juj juj frf juj frf juj
10 f t f t ft ft ftf ftf j y j y jy jy jyj jyj ftf jyj ftf jyj

3 HOME AND FIRST ROW

11 a z a z az az aza aza ; / ; / ;/ ;/ ;/; ;/; aza ;/; aza ;/;
12 s x s x sx sx sxs sxs l . l . l. l. l.l l.l sxs l.l sxs l.l
13 d c d c dc dc dcd dcd k , k , k, k, k,k k,k dcd k,k dcd k,k
14 f v f v fv fv fvf fvf j m j m jm jm jmj jmj fvf jmj fvf jmj
15 f b f b fb fb fbf fbf j n j n jn jn jnj jnj fbf jnj fbf jnj

4 ALL ROWS OF LETTERS

16 aqaza ;p;/; swsxs lol.l dedcd kik,k frftfgfbfvf jujyjhjnjmj
17 a;qpa;z/a; slwoslx.sl dkeidkc,dk fjrufjvmfj fjtyfjghfj bnfj

| 1 | 2 | 3 | 4 | 5 | 6 | 7 | 8 | 9 | 10 | 11 | 12

SI: 1.53

Take 1-minute timings on each paragraph before taking 3-minute timings on the entire page.

15   Today, historians relate that, as a general rule, buy- 12
ing and selling securities was very much unorganized before 24
the year 1792. Every person who owned a security faced the 36
problem of finding interested buyers who might consider the 48
purchase of a debt-free investment. This meant most people 60
were somewhat slow in investing in stocks and bonds because 72
these securities could not readily be converted into money. 84

16   We have been told that an interested number of traders 12 96
and merchants agreed to try to do something to help correct 24 108
the situation. At this first crucial meeting, they decided 36 120
that it was a good idea to visit regularly on a daily basis 48 132
to buy and to sell securities. The group of leaders, whose 60 144
meeting place was under an old, tall cottonwood tree, found 72 156
the needed time to plot the financial future of our nation. 84 168

17   We know from reading the old records that the original 12 180
team who met together long ago in May became the very first 24 192
members of the New York Stock Exchange. The New York Stock 36 204
Exchange is still operating. Other stock exchanges conduct 48 216
business in many countries around the world. Thousands and 60 228
thousands of stocks and bonds are bought and sold each day. 72 240

| 1 | 2 | 3 | 4 | 5 | 6 | 7 | 8 | 9 | 10 | 11 | 12

DRILLS

Use these drills selectively. They are only valuable if you need improvement in the specific technique indicated.

5 TO SHARPEN STROKING/ SPACING

Spacing: Use a light, quick down-and-in motion.

```
1  aj ak al a; la ls ld lf sj sk sl s; ka ks kd kf dj dk dl d;    12
2  fj fk fl f; ja js jd jf gh gk gl g; ha hs hd hf ask lad had    24

3  frf juj ded kik sws lol aqa ;p; ftf jyj free jeer deed good    36
4  fvf jmj dcd k,k sxs l.l aza ;/; fbf jnj zinc lamb cave jamb    48

5  Hal said he had to go into the big city early the next day.  12 12
6  May was glad she and her friends had joined the micro club.  12 24
7  I need to buy a treat for our puppy when I go to the store.  12 36
8  Errors are easy to correct when typing on my microcomputer.  12 48
```

6 TO REDUCE HAND BOUNCING

The vertical lines mark off the phrases; do not type the lines.

```
9   add ask had has lad dad sad ads all gas sag jag fad hah lag    12
10  half dash lass fall dads alga asks lads glad lags saga fads    24
11  shall salad falls sagas halls slags lads; glad; lags; dads;    36
12  a lad|a fad|a dad|a sad|a lass|a dash|a fall|a saga|a half;    48
13  a; a lad; a lad had; a sad lad had; a sad lad had a mad fad    60

14  Ada adds a dash of class as a lass and lads fall in a hall.  12 12
15  Al shall ask all dads to ask my lads to bring half a salad.  12 24
16  A lass shall ask a glad lad to add a fall ad about my saga.  12 36
```

```
|  1  |  2  |  3  |  4  |  5  |  6  |  7  |  8  |  9  |  10  |  11  |  12
```

NORMAL MATERIAL

SI: 1.38

Take 1-minute timings on each paragraph before taking 3-minute timings on the entire page.

12   One morning my friend and I were thinking about how we   12
could plan our summer break away from school. Driving from   24
our own state to several nearby states would help to expand   36
our limited funds. Inviting six other friends to accompany   48
us would lower our car expenses. Stopping at certain sites   60
would also help us stretch our truly limited travel budget.   72

13   Yesterday I engaged in an interesting and enlightening   12   84
discussion about finances. I found it difficult to imagine   24   96
that during my lifetime I might well earn at least one-half   36 108
million dollars. It is also possible that I might spend as   48 120
much as one-half million during this same time period. The   60 132
really difficult thing for me to do will be to save more of   72 144
the half-million than I spend. Thinking about today's high   84 156
cost of living makes this seem an impossible task for most.   96 168

14   Last week I asked a friend to talk with me and a girl-   12 180
friend about college. Our friend is the Dean of Women at a   24 192
nearby college. The Dean and her staff spend much of their   36 204
time talking to students who plan to go on to college. The   48 216
first thing she said was to work very hard each day in high   60 228
school. Good grades are most important for being accepted.   72 240
Being on time for classes and having a good view toward all   84 252
phases of the school life are two other things to remember.   96 264

| 1 | 2 | 3 | 4 | 5 | 6 | 7 | 8 | 9 | 10 | 11 | 12

7 TO RAISE LOW WRISTS

17	you pit yip par your type riot trot quiet peony piety trite	12
18	our toy row due pert ripe they typo route truly perky troop	24
19	tow due two are whet poor owed peer quite topic petty tutor	36
20	pot wit new buy port poor rite pier rotor quota tower error	12 48
21	poi top urn the whey rote rope pity trout piper rerun peeve	24 60
22	wet too red who quit poet tire wipe equip towel rupee trier	36 72
23	You truly tire of wiping our toy tower with your wet towel.	12 12
24	Ruthe Pruitt owed Putt quite a lot of money for his poetry.	12 24

8 TO LOWER HIGH WRISTS

25	nib cam mob nab buzz mean onyx name venom comma vixen maze,	12
26	abb vim con mix zany jazz lynx baby cabby verve conic vice,	24
27	can ban cub mom czar mime zinc vane annex bobby bacon beck,	36
28	cox bib mum box bomb came vain acne combs canny cynic navy,	12 48
29	cab bin nun bum numb curb exam back xebec civic cubic cave,	24 60
30	vex bob bun men minx next oxen cane zombi comic nanny main,	36 72
31	Mom named the baby lynx cub, but a mob of cynics nabbed it.	12 12
32	Vain Buzz blows sax in my zany jazz band in the next annex.	12 24

| 1 | 2 | 3 | 4 | 5 | 6 | 7 | 8 | 9 | 10 | 11 | 12 |

SI: 1.30

Take 1-minute timings on each paragraph before taking 3-minute timings on the entire page.

9   Trying to make a wise, good choice when thinking about   12
what kinds of careers might be best for you is a hard thing   24
to do. Your future may very well depend on the ways you go   36
about finding the best job openings for you in the world of   48
work. Some people will feel that there is one and only one   60
job in the world for them. Hard thinking and a lot of hard   72
work will help them find the one job that is best for them.   84
Jobs are there for those with skills and a good work ethic.   96

10   Many new young artists in the upper New England states   12 108
are famous around the world as leaders in new American art.   24 120
These fine artists are very good in their chosen fields and   36 132
are willing to share their many talents by teaching others.   48 144
The students have had the chance to learn and use skills in   60 156
oil painting, sketching with chalk, sculpting, and weaving.   72 168

11   Learning to typewrite is a skill that will help all of   12 180
us in our work today. The development of the computer will   24 192
open doors for people with keyboarding skills and will make   36 204
typing a necessity. Managers, as well as secretaries, will   48 216
need skill at the keyboard to input data and process words.   60 228
Therefore, good keyboarding skills may be important to you.   72 240

| 1 | 2 | 3 | 4 | 5 | 6 | 7 | 8 | 9 | 10 | 11 | 12

D<u>RILL</u>S

9 FIRST FINGERS

Pretest/
Posttest

Practice

10 SECOND FINGERS

Pretest/
Posttest

Practice

These drills will help strengthen each finger's control of its keys. Take a 1-minute timing on the Pretest. Practice the drill lines for 3 to 5 minutes. Then take the Posttest.

1	Guy hugged and rubbed the grubby mutt when it tried to run.	12
2	fff fgf frf ftf fff fvf fbf fff fgf frf ftf fff fvf fbf fff	12
3	jjj jhj juj jyj jjj jmj jnj jjj jhj juj jyj jjj jmj jnj jjj	24
4	ggf rrf ttf vvf bbf frrf juuj fttf jyyj fvvf jmmj fbbf jnnj	36
5	hhj uuj yyj mmj nnj fggf jhhj frvf jumj ftbf jynj gtbf hynj	48
6	tub hum buy try nut runt buff jury ruby grub bunt numb hurt	60
7	frrf juuj fttf jyyj fvbf jmnj frfvf jujmj ftfbf jyjnj fgjhf	72
8	tuft hunt turn bury fury hung funny buggy truth gummy tubby	84

9	Eddie Eide kidded, and he decided Ike kicked the iced deck.	12
10	ddd ded ddd dcd ddd ded ede ede eee ddd dcd cdc cdc ccc ddd	12
11	kkk kik kkk k,k kkk kik iki iki iii kkk k,k ,k, ,k, ,,, kkk	24
12	dkd ded kik dcd k,k deed kiik dccd k,,k decd ki,k dced k,ik	36
13	did die ice eke kid iced kick deed deck cede died dike eked	48
14	deed kiik dccd k,,k dced k,ik dedcd kik,k dcded k,kik dck,d	60
15	ice, eke, die, did, kid, ide, kick, dike, eked, deed, cede,	72

| 1 | 2 | 3 | 4 | 5 | 6 | 7 | 8 | 9 | 10 | 11 | 12

SI: 1.20

Take 1-minute timings on each paragraph before taking 3-minute timings on the entire page.

5   The bikers rode down the long and narrow path to reach 12
the city park. When they reached a good spot to rest, they 24
began to look for signs of spring. The sun was bright, and 36
a lot of bright red and blue blooms proved to all that warm 48
spring days were the very best. Spring rides were planned. 60

6   They had a burger at the lake and then rode farther up 12 72
the mountain. As one rider started to get off his bike, he 24 84
slipped and fell. One of the other bikers saw him fall but 36 96
could do nothing to help him. Neither the boy nor the bike 48 108
got hurt. After a brief stop, everyone was ready to go on. 60 120

7   All the bikers enjoyed the nice view when they came to 12 132
the top. All the roads far below them looked like ribbons. 24 144
A dozen or so boats could be seen on the lake. It was very 36 156
quiet and peaceful and no one wished to leave. As they set 48 168
out on their return, they all enjoyed the ease of pedaling. 60 180

8   The bikers came upon a new bike trail. This route led 12 192
to scenery far grander than that seen from the normal path. 24 204
The end of the day brought laughs and cheers from everyone. 36 216
The fact that each person was very, very tired did not keep 48 228
anyone from eagerly planning for the exciting ride to come. 60 240

| 1 | 2 | 3 | 4 | 5 | 6 | 7 | 8 | 9 | 10 | 11 | 12

11 THIRD FINGERS

Pretest/ Posttest

16 Sol sings low solos slowly for Oslo in his wholly wool sox.   12

Practice

17 sss sws sss sxs sss sws wsw wsw www sss sxs xsx xsx xxx sss   12
18 lll lol lll l.l lll lol olo olo ooo lll l.l .l. .l. ... lll   24

19 sls sws lol sxs l.l swws lool sxxs l..l swxs lo.l sxws l.ol   36
20 low sox wow lox sow slow wows lows wool woos solo sows loll   48

21 swws lool sxxs l..l sxws l.ol swsxs lol.l sxsws l.lol sxl.s   60
22 sow. wow. sox. low. lox. woo. solo. sows. slow. loll. wool.   72

12 FOURTH FINGERS

Pretest/ Posttest

23 Lazy papa zapped a prize quail; it ran crazily to the maze.   12

Practice

24 aaa aqa aaa aza aaa aqa qaq qaq qqq aaa aza zaz zaz zzz aaa   12
25 ;;; ;p; ;;; ;/; ;;; ;p; p;p p;p ppp ;;; ;/; /;/ /;/ /// ;;;   24

26 a;a aqa ;p; aza ;/; aqqa ;pp; azza ;//; aqza ;p/; azqa ;/p;   36
27 quo zap qua pap apa pica lazy qual papa zips opal quip gaze   48

28 aqqa ;pp; azza ;//; azqa ;/p; aqaza ;p;/; azaqa ;/;p; az;/a   60
29 zap; quo/ pap; qua/ apa; zip/ papa; quip/ aqua; hazy/ maze;   72

| 1 | 2 | 3 | 4 | 5 | 6 | 7 | 8 | 9 | 10 | 11 | 12 |

CONTROLLED-PARAGRAPH

D̲RILL̲S

Use the easy paragraphs to increase your speed. Use the other paragraphs to stabilize your new rate so that you can readily type copy of ordinary difficulty at your new rate.

163 VERY EASY MATERIAL

SI: 1.15

Take 1-minute timings on each paragraph before taking 3-minute timings on the whole page.

1 Jim and Anne will be in charge of the spring field day 12
to be held in early June. They will ask their friends' aid 24
to get set up. There will be games for the boys and girls. 36
The children will want to hike, ride their bikes, and swim. 48
This yearly event will be held in the new Peach Grove Park. 60

2 Ruth has work to do on the plans for food for the day. 12 72
Last year Ruth spent most of her time helping the two cooks 24 84
with many snacks. Hot dogs, fries, soft drinks, ice cream, 36 96
and candy apples were big sellers. Apple pie and ice cream 48 108
sold well too. I hope Ruth serves the same food this year. 60 120

3 George Long will hire the band and singer for the day. 12 132
A great jazz band will play. George's mom leads the group. 24 144
The jazz band is sure to be one of the big hits. George is 36 156
to have them play from one to four and also in the evening. 48 168
The fine songs they will play are sure to please all of us. 60 180

4 Nice gifts will be given to all of the winners in each 12 192
of the events. Local news coverage will include television 24 204
and newspapers. Joyce Scott will take care of the pictures 36 216
for the school paper and yearbook. Maybe the national news 48 228
will do a short story on the tenth annual spring field day. 60 240

| 1 | 2 | 3 | 4 | 5 | 6 | 7 | 8 | 9 | 10 | 11 | 12

13 ALTERNATE-HAND SENTENCES

Take a 1-minute Pretest on each section. Rank timings B and C in order of difficulty. If B is more difficult: practice B drill lines for 3 minutes, C drill lines for 2 minutes. If C is more difficult: practice C drill lines for 3 minutes, B drill lines for 2 minutes.

Pretest A

#		
1	Henry may make a big profit with the rocks by their island.	12
2	Blanche works with their neighbor for the big antique firm.	24
3	Nancy paid them for their signs with eight bushels of corn.	36

Pretest B
Shifting
(Followed by letter in shifting hand)

#		
4	Jeanie and Rodney did go to Malaysia to visit Hank and Bob.	12
5	Shelby Orland did go to Japan and Ghana with Larry Borland.	24
6	Did Burlene pay Duane and Henry for their Big Island audit?	36

Pretest C
Shifting
(Followed by letter in opposite hand)

#		
7	Norma and Raley make Indian bowls for Normandy and Midland.	12
8	Myra and Norman Daniels work for Bennington Associates Inc.	24
9	Bengie Salcorn asked Wendle Norman to visit Bali with John.	36

Practice B

#		
10	Quin Jerry Amana Mavis Turkey Oriole Richey Jeanie Williams	12
11	Enid Provo Susan Heidi Austin Marnie Sidney Helena Collette	24
12	Andy Irene Doris Henry Robert Yvonne Eloise Jackie Charlene	36

Practice C

#		
13	Gwen Nordy Benji India Barbra Norman Carole Horton Brigetta	12
14	Sara Nicki Freda Holly Bangor Monica Athena Lowell Franklyn	24
15	Kirk Wayne Milly Debra Johnny George Hilary Denise Kimberly	36

Posttest

Repeat the Pretests.

| 1 | 2 | 3 | 4 | 5 | 6 | 7 | 8 | 9 | 10 | 11 | 12 |

162 TYPING FROM HAND-WRITTEN COPY

Use the paragraphs on page 82 for accurate scoring.

A modern office depends upon a wide variety of written documents. The accuracy of written business communications contributes to efficiency among business workers. Yet each day many errors go undetected, causing waste and confusion. Higher operating costs are a result of all careless errors. 12 24 36 48 60

Many employers now feel accuracy is the most important guide for evaluating work. Speed of work is ranked second. 72 84

Proofreading demands a thorough review of handwritten, typed, or printed matter to find errors needing correction. Proofreaders can develop the skill to locate mechanical and content errors. Mechanical errors are those made in typing or writing — mistakes in word division, spacing, and format. Content errors affect the meaning of the copy and can cause confusion and misinterpretation by the unsuspecting reader. 96 108 120 132 144 156 168

A good proofreader will proofread copy before removing the paper, use the paper bail to keep eyes on the line, and read each line from right to left instead of the usual way. Proofreading is a vital skill that can and must be learned. 180 192 204 216

14 TAB AND MARGIN RELEASE

Take one 1-minute Pretest on each section below.

Pretest 1

Use an *exact* 60-space line. Set a 5-space paragraph indention. (Pica margin settings: 12 and 72; elite margin settings: 20 and 80.)

```
                    ↓ TAB
↓ MARGIN A person does get into a habit of handling business in    12
a certain manner.  The airplane has become the favorite way        24
to travel for many people.  Long distances mean very little        36
to plane travelers.  Imagine the distress they might suffer        48
if fog conditions forced them to spend seven or eight hours        60
on the bus or train instead of about one hour on the plane.        72
```

| 1 | 2 | 3 | 4 | 5 | 6 | 7 | 8 | 9 | 10 | 11 | 12

Pretest 2

Change the right margin setting (pica: 64, elite: 72). Retype the paragraph above. Use the margin release to complete each line.

Pretest 3

Do not change margin settings. Delete the tab for paragraph indention. Five tab stops should be set at 10-space intervals. Use the margin release to complete each line.

```
↓ MARGIN     ↓ TAB       ↓ TAB       ↓ TAB       ↓ TAB       ↓ TAB
amend        blame       chair       civic       corps       cubic     12
cycle        disks       ducks       field       fight       firms     24
forms        fuels       giant       girls       gowns       handy     36
incur        ivory       panel       proxy       right       risks     48
rocks        shelf       sight       signs       spend       lapel     60
their        tight       title       usual       visit       world     72
```

Practice drills are on the next page.

161 **TYPING FROM EDITED COPY**

Use the paragraphs on page 82 for accurate scoring.

a modern of fice depends upon a wide variety of written   12
documents. The accuracy of all written business communicatoins   24
contributes to the efficiency among business workers. Yet each   36
many day errors go undetected, causing waste and confusion.   48
High operating costs are a result of all careless errors.   60

Many employees feel now accuracy is the most important   72
guide for evaluating work. Speed flo work is ranked second.   84

proofreading demands a thorough review of hand written,   96
typed, or printed matter to find errors needing correction.   108
Proofreaders can develop the skill to find locate mechanical and   120
content errors. A mechancial error are those madde in typing   132
or writing--mistakes in work division, spacing, and format.   144
Content errors affect the meaning of the copy can and cause   156
confusion and misinterpretation by the unsuspection readers.   168

a good proofraeder will proofread copy before removing   180
the paper, use the paper bail to keep your eyes on the line, and   192
read all each line from right to left instead of the unusual way.   204
Proofreading is a vital skill that can and must be learned.   216

| 1 | 2 | 3 | 4 | 5 | 6 | 7 | 8 | 9 | 10 | 11 | 12 |

Practice 1

Do not change margin settings or tab stops! Use the margin release to complete each line.

↓ MARGIN	↓ TAB	↓ TAB	↓ TAB	↓ TAB	↓ TAB	
did	auto	burnt	jam	hair	theme	11
man	owns	right	wit	sick	flaps	22
cow	clan	blend	foe	halt	vigor	33
bus	rush	shape	sue	them	focus	44
not	fish	dials	eye	coal	vivid	55

Practice 2

Do not change margin settings. Clear the second and fourth tab stops. Use the margin release to complete each line.

↓ MARGIN	↓ TAB	↓ TAB	↓ TAB	
maps	eight	mantle	ancient	12
burn	laugh	orient	bowling	23
chap	goals	profit	element	35
rock	whale	author	antique	46
sign	towns	emblem	clement	58

Practice 3

Do not change margin settings or tab stops!

Don't forget to indent at the left margin.

↓ MARGIN	↓ TAB	↓ TAB	↓ TAB	
→	did tune	did fight	did signal	13
	for them	for firms	for theory	25
	and held	and visit	and formal	38
	the sock	the chair	the turkey	50
	but wish	but right	but handle	63

Posttest

Repeat the Pretests on page 8.

160 TYPING FROM STRAIGHT COPY

A modern office depends upon a wide variety of written documents. The accuracy of written business communications contributes to efficiency among business workers. Yet each day many errors go undetected, causing waste and confusion. Higher operating costs are a result of all careless errors.

Many employers now feel accuracy is the most important guide for evaluating work. Speed of work is ranked second.

Proofreading demands a thorough review of handwritten, typed, or printed matter to find errors needing correction. Proofreaders can develop the skill to locate mechanical and content errors. Mechanical errors are those made in typing or writing—mistakes in word division, spacing, and format. Content errors affect the meaning of the copy and can cause confusion and misinterpretation by the unsuspecting reader.

A good proofreader will proofread copy before removing the paper, use the paper bail to keep eyes on the line, and read each line from right to left instead of the usual way. Proofreading is a vital skill that can and must be learned.

12
24
36
48
60
72
84
96
108
120
132
144
156
168
180
192
204
216

| 1 | 2 | 3 | 4 | 5 | 6 | 7 | 8 | 9 | 10 | 11 | 12

Take two 3-minute Pretests on the following alphabetic sentences. (If you type more than 48 words a minute, continue on to the next page.) Record the more accurate of the two timings. After completing the drill work on the entire alphabet (pages 12–25), repeat these sentences as your Posttest.

**15 ALPHABETIC
SENTENCES**

(Do not type the
sentence numbers.)

1 Mufi quickly realized which travel posters bring extra joy.   12

2 Philip Godwin acquired my five extra bronze velvet jackets.   24

3 Big jazzy crafts moved expertly over quiet Lake Washington.   36

4 Baking an extra five dozen juicy quiche pies would tire me. 12 48

5 Kevin Max writes prized journals of high quality for clubs. 24 60

6 Jinx gave a few marvelous banquets in cozy Hyde Park homes. 36 72

7 The bold majority was voting to equalize export of chicken. 12 84

8 Quiet Mike plays goofy clarinet with five Dixie jazz bands. 24 96

9 Pretty Delores quickly bought five extra wigwams in Juarez. 36 108

10 Bejay recognized exotic quince while passing my five docks. 12 120

11 Banquet voices buzzed with joyful excitement for kind Page. 24 132

12 The jury acquitted Zelma Buck of excessive puzzling wrongs. 36 144

    | 1 | 2 | 3 | 4 | 5 | 6 | 7 | 8 | 9 | 10 | 11 | 12

156 CAPITALIZATION

Insert 35 capitals.

1	dean asked may and le ann to see joe on friday in new york.	12
2	meet mr. and mrs. max r. green jr. of santa fe, new mexico.	24
3	dr. s. l. reed earned a ph.d. at washington state last may.	36
4	aunt irene and uncle buck saw millie and father in houston.	48

157 SPELLING

Spell all numbers.

5	We need 2 tables, 6 chairs, 1 desk, and 9 carpets.	12
6	Add 6 dates, 4 oranges, 5 plums, and 8 bananas.	24
7	6 boys on 2 teams won 1st and 3rd places on Friday.	36
8	5 or 6 men drove 10 cars in 6 states in 7 days.	48

158 PUNCTUATION

Insert 24 punctuation marks.

9	However Mr C J Gray manager may fly to Salem Oregon	12
10	You too can fly however Nancy please arrive on Sunday	24
11	Yes Mrs Johnson you may leave when your luggage arrives	36
12	On May 2 1984 Paul Sam and Joe will go to Reno Nevada	48

159 ROUGH-DRAFT COPY

Make all corrections.

13	You are developing good typing te^ch niques at your keyboard?	12
14	Go(o)d posture ^improves a typist's accuracy and productivity.	24
15	Keep yuor back str^aight with the your feet firmly on the floor.	36
16	your fingers should be curved slightly as you hit the keys.	48

| 1 | 2 | 3 | 4 | 5 | 6 | 7 | 8 | 9 | 10 | 11 | 12

ALPHABETIC SENTENCES (Continued)

13 Jack objectively examined prize aquarium fish with Grandma. 12

14 Holly Pike was fixing my unique adjectives and crazy verbs. 24

15 Big Vic Knox zealously performs jury duty with quiet class. 36

16 The judges quickly absolved the crazy man of swiping foxes. 12 48

17 Mary Kimmel joined us to explore big white caves of quartz. 24 60

18 Kirby played mighty fine sax with the Victory Jazz Quartet. 36 72

19 Kimberly recognized the export volume for unique wine jars. 12 84

20 Ryan Bille lazily explored quiet caves after a joking whim. 24 96

21 Nine excited journalists flew high over Mozambique Parkway. 36 108

22 Pa wants my big fuzzy jacket or his expensive quilted vest. 12 120

23 Kit and Bob have acquired my five expensive jigsaw puzzles. 24 132

24 Happy Muf seized quick lively jaguars at the new Bronx Zoo. 36 144

25 My five dozen big pickle jars quickly exploded with relish. 12 156

26 Fay Kolb viewed acquired prejudices with amazing expertise. 24 168

27 Jovial Phyllis and Hawk frequently go to Mexico and Brazil. 36 180

| 1 | 2 | 3 | 4 | 5 | 6 | 7 | 8 | 9 | 10 | 11 | 12

1 This 150% increase means the difference between 4¢ and 10¢!   12
2 Jo read <u>Business News</u> by Hill & Clark.   See summary below.*   24
3 The invoice of 7/17 for $82 includes a 2/10, n/30 discount.   36

4 Catalog #327 lists 5 @ 7¢, 35 @ 72¢, 68 @ 10¢, and 9 @ 46¢.   12 48
5 License #21479 from T&M allows a 10% discount on 20# paper.   24 60
6 A salary <u>bonus</u> of 24% announced by Todd & Moe was welcomed.   36 72

7 That teacher feels ¼ + ¼, ½ + ½, and ½ + ¼ are easy to add.   12 84
8 The 15% increase in costs required M&Z to raise prices 10%.   24 96
9 On 12/30 the Hartly Company* stock decreased 10 1/8 points!   36 108

10 J&J fixed our roof at 15½ Plum St.   <u>Total</u> cost was $980.98.   12 120
11 We bought 28# of nuts/bolts @ 98¢, an increase of over 39%.   24 132
12 Wow!   Get that report* at C&G!   Buy four copies @ 98¢ each.   36 144

13 I know that 2 + 2 = 4, 3 + 3 = 6, 4 + 4 = 8, and 5 + 4 = 9.   12 156
14 On 12/16/84 he got 29# of bricks @ 35¢, an increase of 27%.   24 168
15 Fantastic!   Our article was published in <u>Business Ed World</u>.   36 180

16 If you use ½ and ¼, please do not mix them with 1/2 or 1/4.   12 192
17 The modest salary of $939 represents an increase of 3 1/5%.   24 204
18 She ordered 350# of #2 potatoes, which retail for 25# @ $8.   36 216

| 1 | 2 | 3 | 4 | 5 | 6 | 7 | 8 | 9 | 10 | 11 | 12

Practice

These lines provide a quick review of the keyboard and excellent practice for accuracy.

16 ALPHABET REVIEW

1 a b c d e f g abcdefg a b c d e f g abcdefg a b c d e f g
2 h i j k l m n hijklmn h i j k l m n hijklmn h i j k l m n
3 o p q r s t u opqrstu o p q r s t u opqrstu o p q r s t u
4 v w x y z vwxyz v w x y z vwxyz v w x y z vwxyz v w x y z

5 abcdefghijklm abcdefghijklm abcdefghijklm abcdefghijklm
6 nopqrstuvwxyz nopqrstuvwxyz nopqrstuvwxyz nopqrstuvwxyz

7 abcd bcde cdef defg efgh fghi ghij hijk ijkl jklm klmn lmno
8 mnop nopq opqr pqrs qrst rstu stuv tuvw uvwx vwxy wxyz abcd

9   a b c d e f g h i j k l m n o p q r s t u v w x y z xyz xyz
10 abcdefghijklmnopqrstuvwxyz zyxwvutsrqponmlkjihgfedcba vwxyz

17 ALPHABETIC 3-LETTER WORDS

All the letters of the alphabet are used in these lines.

11 vex bay cod dig elf fur gab his ilk jaw kit zip mix nun qua   12
12 pen qui rot sap keg vat wax lay zap hum bed joy fun end cad   24
13 bud axe hot sir let cam quo vet own zoo ado yet kip jig fit   36

14 ban quo mud wet fix gum sop coy zag job her via lot kid put 12 48
15 met led gym pig now sit zoa bat cub eve fox jar kit hew qui 24 60
16 quo viz jay hag mix nor cab dot foe ask lop win sun two and 36 72

| 1 | 2 | 3 | 4 | 5 | 6 | 7 | 8 | 9 | 10 | 11 | 12

151 ¢ SIGN

The ¢ sign is used to express *cents*.

29 jjj jyj j6j j6j 666 j6¢ j6¢ j¢j ¢j¢ 6¢6 ¢6¢ j¢j j6j j6¢ j¢j 12
30 j6¢j j6¢j j¢¢j for 6¢ for 8¢ for 2¢ for 19¢ for 10¢ for 23¢ 24
31 We bid on 300 at 27¢, 122 at 18¢, 42 at 11¢, and 15 at 96¢. 12

152 / SIGN

The / sign is called *diagonal*.

32 ;;; ;/; ;/; /// ;/; ;;; ;/; ;/; /;/ ;/; /;/ /;/ ;/; ;/; /;/ 12
33 She/he you/yours they/them and/or to/from 10/19/70 12/25/90 24
34 He/she will provide his/her report on 10/31/84 or 11/25/84. 12

153 ½ AND ¼

Fraction key ¼ is the shift of the ½ key.

Other fractions are made using the diagonal. Do not mix styles.

35 ;;; ;½; ;;; ;½; ;½; ½;½ ½;½ ;½; ;¼; ;¼; ¼;¼ ¼;¼ ;¼; ;½¼ ;½¼ 12
36 and ½ and ¼ add ¼ and ¼ add ½ and ¼ add ½ and ½ and ¼ and ¼ 24
37 Add 1½ and 1½ Add 2¼ and 2¼ Add 3½ and 4¼ Add ¼ and ½ and ¼ 36
38 My recipe needs 2½ cups flour, 1¼ cups sugar, and ½ t salt. 12
39 1/5, 2/7, 7/8, 3/10, 4 4/5, 3 3/13, 26 2/15, 18 2/3, 1 1/16 12
40 Add 3/8 and 2/5. Add 6/9 and 2/5. Add 2/9, 2/7, and 4/89. 24
41 Math students add 3/5, 7 1/2, 56 1/4, 70 4/9, and 48 19/26. 12

154 SPECIAL KEYS

The ! is the shift of the 1 key.

= and +
Use these symbols if your machine has them.

42 aaa aqa ala ala a!a al! al! a!a !a! l!l !l! a!a ala al! a!a 12
43 Wow! Hah! Alas! Oh no! Please! Not now! Not 1! Or 2! 24
44 Hurry! Hurry! Fantastic bargains! Our sale ends Tuesday! 12
45 ;;; ;=; ;=; =;= ;;; ;=; ;+; ;+; ;=; ;+; ;=+ ;=+ ;+; ;+; ;=+ 12
46 12 + 12 = 24|9 + 9 = 18|7 + 7 + 7 = 21|3 + 3 = 6|5 + 5 = 10 24
47 The sum of 3 + 3 = 6, 2 + 2 = 4, 1 + 1 = 2, and 4 + 7 = 11. 12

| 1 | 2 | 3 | 4 | 5 | 6 | 7 | 8 | 9 | 10 | 11 | 12

18 ALPHABETIC 4-LETTER WORDS

17   aqua work gave mist apex yolk neck hide zips joke fire best   12

18   bank calf knit move jogs axle quay wait arid zany opal hope   24

19   itch jump frog quad bite walk navy slot zero jest coax deal   36

20   calm quiz hold easy bait rope give wart jinx duck fate jury 12   48

21   balk evil deep year omen zinc figs hoax jerk quit want post 24   60

22   cast quip drum yoke bevy axis fine zeal gust hour jaws awry 36   72

19 ALPHABETIC 5-LETTER WORDS

23   bayou waxed faith quiet corps zebra junky novel gloat maxim 12   84

24   wharf model jerky xebec pilot value zones yacht graft quote 24   96

25   blaze globe dozen skier cloth weave jumpy quart exact faint 36   108

26   quake major blind fixed hairy trick genie waltz valid usurp 12   120

27   dimly squab joker czars lowly ghost yeast vixen piers fable 24   132

28   batch women ivory quick excel fazed vigor jewel halve super 36   144

20 ALPHABETIC NAMES

29   Chuck Walt Rex Jason Quin Dom Patsy Inez Gay Bobby Marv Jef 12   156

30   Hazel Marg Wes Vince Jake Fay Quinn Beth Dot Patty Cary Max 24   168

31   Polly Quen May Kirby Jane Dan Tasha Gwen Vic Freda Roxy Zoe 36   180

32   Wally Faye Jim Quint Hope Dex Joyce Russ Guy Vicki Zeke Bev 48   192

| 1 | 2 | 3 | 4 | 5 | 6 | 7 | 8 | 9 | 10 | 11 | 12

147 & SIGN

The & sign is called *ampersand*.

13 jjj juj j7j j7j 777 j7& j7& j&j &j& 7&7 &7& j&j j7j j7& j&j 12

14 j77j j77j j7&j j7&j j&&j j7&j j7&j j77j j7&j j7&7 j7&7 j&j& 24

15 1 & 2 & j&j ss&s B&O AT&T |hill & dale|back & forth|to & fro 36

16 Jo worked at A&P, AT&T, and B&O before going to Hill & Poe. 12

148 * SIGN

The * sign is called *asterisk*.

17 kkk kik k8k k8k 888 k8* k8* k*k *k* 8*8 *8* k*k k8k k8* k*k 12

18 k88k k88k k8*k k8*k k**k k8*k k8*k k88k k8*8 k8*8 k8*8 k*k* 24

19 Long* Wold* Jones* Bille* *Smith said *See table *See below 36

20 The asterisk, *, is used to indicate a footnote* reference. 12

149 _ MARK

The underscore is the shift of the hyphen.

21 ;;; ;p; ;-; ;-; --- ;-- ;__ ;__ _;_ ___ ___ ;_; ;-; ;__ ;-; 12

22 ;--; ;--; ;__; ;_; ;__; ;--; ;_; ;--; ;__; ;--; ;__; ;_;_ 24

23 in 11 and 12 and 13 and 14 and 15 Time Newsweek The Journal 36

24 He wrote articles for Time, Newsweek, and The Morning News. 12

150 @ SIGN

The @ sign is used to express *at* or *at a rate of*.

25 sss sws s2s s2s 222 s2@ s2@ s@s @s@ 2@2 @2@ s@s s2s s2@ s@s 12

26 s22s s22s s2@s s2@s s@@s s2@s s2@s s22s s2@2 s2@2 s2@2 s@s@ 24

27 32 @ |16 @ |27 @ |44 @ |92 @ |14 @ |80 @ |54 @ |61 @ |1 @ $7 |2 @ $83 36

28 She purchased 7 @ $4, 3 @ $25, 6 @ $9, 2 @ $83, and 1 @ $1. 12

| 1 | 2 | 3 | 4 | 5 | 6 | 7 | 8 | 9 | 10 | 11 | 12

21 ALPHABETIC SENTENCES

"OK" timings: Must be errorless for 30 seconds.

Make a special effort to keep elbows in and wrists low.

1 Zak was given a free smallpox vaccine by the jealous squad.   12

2 Big Alex quickly drank five whole cups of zesty plum juice.   24

3 Gaby Koch will adjust my quota level for Cadiz expeditions.   36

4 Just fifty hands were picked to excavate my blazing quarry.   12 48

5 Pat Wolfe has judged very excellent bronze antique monkeys.   24 60

6 Jovial Debra Frantz swims quickly with grace and expertise.   36 72

7 Margy fixed five dozen jonquil baskets with pretty candles.   12 84

8 Jack Quigley poorly reviewed many fine exhibits at the zoo.   24 96

9 Dwight Ek explores amazing folklore movies in jolly Quebec.   36 108

10 An excited jumpy fish zoomed quickly by this viewing perch.   12 120

11 The expert Bolivian jockey was jumping four unique hazards.   24 132

12 Chub Maxwell quietly served pizza to a gang of jovial kids.   36 144

13 The plump wizard converted junk boxes to quality feed bags.   12 156

14 Mike Bingham was saving old crazy jars for antique experts.   24 168

15 Lizzy brought six cans wrapped in jute from Iraq for Vicky.   36 180

| 1 | 2 | 3 | 4 | 5 | 6 | 7 | 8 | 9 | 10 | 11 | 12 |

SYMBOL DRILLS

When typing a symbol, follow these simple steps: (1) shift, (2) strike the symbol, and (3) return your finger to the home row. Make the reach without moving your hand down for the shift key or up for the symbol key.

144 # SIGN

sign before the number reads *number.*

sign after the number reads *pounds.*

```
1   d33d d33d d3#d d3#d d##d d3#d d3#d d33d d3#3 d3#3 d3#3 d#d#      24
2   #333 #373 #283 #162 #746 #931 #362 #175 #433 #659 #702 #683      36
3   333# 263# 174# 936# 607# 657# 849# 372# 946# 107# 789# 616#      48
4   I need 2# of #3 nails, 7# of #6 bolts, and 58# of #9 clips.      12
```

145 $ SIGN

```
5   f44f f44f f4$f f4$f f$$f f4$f f4$f f44f f4$4 f4$4 f4$4 f$f$      24
6   $444 $474 $284 $164 $746 $391 $702 $731 $495 $554 $328 $620      36
7   $1.23 $7.34 $3.45 $4.56 $5.67 $5.78 $7.89 $8.90 $9.10 $1.63      48
8   I owed $2.29, Jo owed $.98, and Lu owed $.76 and paid $.24.      12
```

146 % SIGN

```
9   f55f f55f f5%f f5%f f%%f f5%f f5%f f55f f5%5 f5%5 f5%5 f%f%      24
10  55% 36% 38% 29% 10% 65% 81% 13% 67% 94% 11% 56% 73% 19% 37%      36
11  73.1% 52.5% 93.2% 64.9% 84.6% 43.4% 10.1% 19.3% 60.4% 32.5%      48
12  Lee received scores of 60%, 71%, 83%, and 94% on the tests.      12

    | 1 | 2 | 3 | 4 | 5 | 6 | 7 | 8 | 9 | 10 | 11 | 12
```

16 Jamison exports a huge quantity of vegetables and zwieback. 12
17 Hurt Buzz Weaver jogged and quickly flexed painful muscles. 24
18 Hazy dark fog quietly covers Wizard Jon as my lab explodes. 36

19 Crazy viewers jumping frequently excite bored hockey idols. 12 48
20 A mock jury acquitted five publicized boxers in Washington. 24 60
21 The panicky Queen of Cadiz was viewing onyx marble jewelry. 36 72

22 Jodie very quickly examined and sewed the big fine zippers. 12 84
23 Victor zipped through quickly but just finished with exams. 24 96
24 Mike Wally acquired visiting exhibits for the Japanese zoo. 36 108

25 Rex enjoys playing with farm ducks by the quiet lazy river. 12 120
26 Freda Hyke was giving six major bronze plaques for casting. 24 132
27 Hal Rex knows bicycling means prize views and joyful quiet. 36 144

28 Jojo frequently publicized expensive hacksaws in magazines. 12 156
29 Jack Baxter followed the gypsy queens to my dozen beehives. 24 168
30 Lazy Jef asked tax questions and rampaged with Vic and Bob. 36 180

| 1 | 2 | 3 | 4 | 5 | 6 | 7 | 8 | 9 | 10 | 11 | 12

Type slowly and evenly. See page 1 for proper body and hand position. See pages 7–9 for additional practice.

139 SPACING

Use a light, quick, down-and-in motion.

```
1  a b c d e f g h i j k l m n o p q r s t u v w x y z a b c d     12
2  z y x w v u t s r q p o n m l k j i h g f e d c b a z y x w     24
```

140 CARRIER RETURN

Type each word on a single line.

```
3  pert ruby once turn puff soap cart null gale limp gone town    12
4  Came Down Cook Even Come Hash Barb Iron Data Inch Odds Book    24
```

141 SHIFTING

In line 7, cap each letter separately.

```
5  aA bB cC dD eE fF gG hH iI jJ kK lL mM nN oO pP qQ rR sS tT     12
6  uU vV wW xX yY zZ Alan Babs Carl Dora Edie Fran Gregg Henry    24
7  HAL DICKS DID WORK FOR THE RIGHT FIRM AND OWNS EIGHT AUTOS.    36
```

142 BACKSPACE/ UNDERSCORE

```
8  Underscoring helps emphasize important words in the report.    25
9  Underline book titles--Exodus, Hawaii, and Grapes of Wrath.    50
```

143 LOCATING CHANGED KEYS

```
10  ;'; ';' ;'; We don't think Robert's plan is what we'd like!   12
11  ;'" ";" ;"; "Yes," mother said, "please call from Croydon."   12
12  k8* *k* k*k One will see the asterisk, *, on the eight key.   12
13  j6¢ ¢j¢ j¢j John ordered 7 for 4¢, 6 for 3¢, and 2 for 14¢.   12
14  s2@ @s@ s@s Buy only 7 @ 26¢, 9 @ 54¢, 8 @ 70¢, and 6 @ 3¢.   12
      |  1  |  2  |  3  |  4  |  5  |  6  |  7  |  8  |  9  |  10  |  11  |  12
```

31 Paddy and Jeb will give many quick extra tours of this zoo. 12
32 Roxy picked five jonquils while Buz stayed with my grandpa. 24
33 Jake expects Ward to acquire seven prize goldfish by March. 36

34 His deft joking brought quizzical expressions to my viewer. 12 48
35 Jed Mak will veto five taxicab zones right on an open quay. 24 60
36 Last week Jacqueline brought Pram five or six lazy donkeys. 36 72

37 Six jovial men on the flying trapeze quake when crowds boo. 12 84
38 Mixing home jobs with office tasks penalized my quiet Vera. 24 96
39 A jury acquitted big Zane Koche of very weird tax problems. 36 108

40 He examined a few subjects and very quickly recognized pox. 12 120
41 Poky Jean acquired six amazing velvet hats with fine braid. 24 132
42 Jacques gave Micky a balloon while we fixed pizza for Todd. 36 144

43 A dozen men quickly jump high to verify codes on wet boxes. 12 156
44 Stephen Finke boxed and gave aquamarine and zircon jewelry. 24 168
45 Mike Cowen qualified the expert jury while visiting Brazil. 36 180

| 1 | 2 | 3 | 4 | 5 | 6 | 7 | 8 | 9 | 10 | 11 | 12

COMPUTER VOCABULARY

DRILLS

135 COMPUTER LANGUAGES

New technology in the computer field is creating a continually expanding vocabulary.

1   RPG | APL | COBOL | PILOT | BASIC | FORTRAN | Pascal | Assembler Language   12

136 BASIC LANGUAGE

Use shift lock to represent computer output.

2   BASIC--the Beginner's All-Purpose Symbolic Instruction Code   24

3   RUN LIST PRINT LET DATA RENUM END READ POINT FOR TAB RETURN   36

4   NEW GOTO INPUT REM NEXT GOSUB DIM EDIT RESET SET CLS DELETE   48

137 COMMON COMPUTER VOCABULARY

5   CPU key data bits input micro coding floppy printer network   60

6   CRT bus disk byte debug break binary string program records   72

7   CAI log menu chip array clear memory branch address scanner   84

8   RAM bug file mode error enter output decode command storage   96

9   ROM run dump flow field modem cursor encode monitor turnkey   108

10   crash keypad software diskette variable processor bootstrap   120

11   digit glitch hardware joystick keyboard flowchart scrolling   132

12   burst search terminal computer magnetic interface computing   144

138 SENTENCES

13   The information processor stores file data on floppy disks.   12   12

14   The BASIC language needs the binary code to translate data.   12   24

| 1 | 2 | 3 | 4 | 5 | 6 | 7 | 8 | 9 | 10 | 11 | 12

Review two letters each day. Practice the first four lines in the section for each letter for 3 minutes. After this practice, take one 1-minute "OK" timing on each sentence following the drill lines (for example, lines 5 and 6 would be used for letter A and 11 and 12 for letter B).

22 THE LETTER A

1	aaa asa aaa ada aaa afa aqa aza aaa aAa AaA Asa Ada Afa aaa	12
2	alas data array adapt attack annual airmail apparel analyze	24
3	saga ajar avail atlas anyway asthma antenna average arrival	36
4	analyst actuators auxiliary characters mainframe wraparound	48

"OK" timings: Typing with no more than 1 error per minute.

5	Azaleas appear as alfalfa as Allan amazes with abracadabra.	12
6	Admirals aboard a naval armada accurately analyze averages.	12

23 THE LETTER B

7	fbf bbb fbf bbb fBf BfB bBb BbB fbf bbb ebb bib Bob Bab bbb	12
8	blab baby bribe abbey bubble hobnob bubonic blabber cobbler	24
9	barb ebbs rabbi nabob busboy bobbed bramble jobbers blubber	36
10	barber bobbing bandbox backbone babbling bobbinet bumblebee	48
11	Rabbits nibble by baby Barbie while bumblebees buzz nearby.	12
12	Blubbering robbers were blamable for bribery and barbarity.	12

| 1 | 2 | 3 | 4 | 5 | 6 | 7 | 8 | 9 | 10 | 11 | 12 |

16 liable hygiene liquefy opinion omission quantity insistence   12
17 nickel labeled mileage panicky parallel relevant irrelevant   24
18 omelet leisure neither pastime patience renowned laboratory   36

19 pursue library offense proceed persuade schedule lieutenant   48
20 resume license offered receipt pretense separate resistance   60
21 rhythm likable oneself receive publicly sergeant hemorrhage   72

22 recruit summary itinerary plausible coincidence permissible   84
23 rescind theater miniature preceding detrimental possessions   96
24 salable through necessary privilege development practically   108

25 sizable totaled negotiate procedure exhaustible prerogative   120
26 sponsor tragedy partially recipient maintenance susceptible   132
27 surgeon whether physician recommend mischievous temperature   144

28 consensus apparently achievement accompanying conscientious   156
29 criticism changeable accommodate accidentally extraordinary   168
30 defendant collateral acquisition acquaintance hors d'oeuvre   180

31 eliminate commitment appreciable advantageous miscellaneous   192
32 embarrass comparison approximate dissatisfied pronunciation   204
33 emphasize conscience psychiatric incidentally psychological   216

| 1 | 2 | 3 | 4 | 5 | 6 | 7 | 8 | 9 | 10 | 11 | 12

24 THE LETTER C

13 dcd ccc dcd ccc dCd CdC cCc CcC dcd ccc car cot Cil Cec ccc 12

14 coco chic occur cinch access concur classic chicken conceit 24
15 coca club catch check crunch circus cascade comical cardiac 36

16 cancel calcium collect economic cucumber accuracy conscious 48

17 Cec acclaims a concise concoction of cucumber and broccoli. 12
18 Precise accrual accounting concerns careful civic councils. 12

25 THE LETTER D

19 ddd dsd ddd dfd ddd dad ded dcd ddd dDd DdD Dom Don Dad ddd 12

20 dyad dido dowdy diode dander divide decoded disdain address 24
21 dado eddy dozed faded dialed decade decided dwindle fiddler 36

22 draped diamond bidding deadline dividend daydream dignified 48

23 Bedridden Dee dozed under eiderdown and dreamed of dancing. 12
24 Eddy is befuddled and disdainful of division and dividends. 12

26 THE LETTER E

25 ded eee ded eee dEd EdE eEe EeE ded eee eel eye Dee Lee eee 12

26 edge eyes event eleven deeded breeze encore decoder deceive 24
27 ease even sweep emerge fewest coffee recede degrees element 36

28 ewe reel reader device encoder pinfeed retrieval electronic 48

29 Geese and egret seek refuge from the severe eastern breeze. 12
30 Empress Ev embedded eleven emeralds into an evergreen tree. 12

| 1 | 2 | 3 | 4 | 5 | 6 | 7 | 8 | 9 | 10 | 11 | 12

The following words are often misspelled. The best way to learn to spell them correctly is through practice.

134 SPELLING WORDS

1 aging across adjacent amortize category acquiesce benefited   12
2 aisle answer attorney analysis cemetery arbitrary committee   24
3 empty autumn boundary argument describe architect conscious   36

4 forty biased calendar bachelor exercise auxiliary enumerate   48
5 gauge column carriage campaign familiar basically existence   60
6 ninth debtor colossal canceled fourteen beginning extension   72

7 phase double absence eligible judgment facsimile assistance   84
8 queue eighth alleged grateful misspell guarantee bankruptcy   96
9 seize exceed analyze grievous mortgage hypocrisy continuous   108

10 siege fourth believe guardian pamphlet innocuous descendant   120
11 suing harass catalog maneuver subpoena inoculate disappoint   132
12 tempt height colonel marriage subtlety supersede dissimilar   144

13 their concede forbade exaggerate occasionally approximately   156
14 title defense foreign exhibition perseverance beneficiaries   168
15 usage deficit foresee exorbitant presumptuous chronological   180

| 1 | 2 | 3 | 4 | 5 | 6 | 7 | 8 | 9 | 10 | 11 | 12

27 THE LETTER F

31 fff fdf fff fsf fff faf frf ftf fvf fbf fff fgf Fat Fad fff   12

32 fife puff huffy fifth buffer affirm fifteen afflict buffalo   24
33 Fifi cuff offer fifty waffle fitful fortify chiffon fistful   36

34 afford fulfill falsify fanciful official faithful plaintiff   48

35 Francis feels iffy about fifteen unofficial office raffles.   12
36 Inefficient officials forgot fifty frankfurters and coffee.   12

28 THE LETTER G

37 fgf ggg fgf ggg fGf fGf fgf ggg gGg GgG ggg Gus Guy Gay ggg   12

38 gang gong foggy gauge giggle haggle trigger garbage Georgia   24
39 grog gags gouge going pegged groggy geology hoggish luggage   36

40 eggs agog piggy gorge soggy gargle garage rigging debugging   48

41 Greg suggests studying geography or geology to Guy and Gay.   12
42 Tagging luggage in the garage makes giggly Georgia haggard.   12

29 THE LETTER H

43 jhj hhh jhj hhh jHj jHj jhj hhh hHh HhH hhh Ham Hon Hal hhh   12

44 hash high hatch heath hurrah hyphen heather hotshot hoggish   24
45 hath hush hutch hitch height hearth highest hibachi Hialeah   36

46 health haggish humbler withhold headache hatchery household   48

47 My haberdasher withheld haircloth from haughty Hannah Hugh.   12
48 A headache has Heath halfheartedly hosing hothouse heather.   12

| 1 | 2 | 3 | 4 | 5 | 6 | 7 | 8 | 9 | 10 | 11 | 12

WORDS (Continued)

14 number during report letter through however request control 12
15 school review amount policy because present section current 24

16 within period future people further contact include several 36
17 return action county public changes problem account subject 48
18 months change annual market forward student working without 60

19 those payment support enclosed business equipment following 72
20 sales members percent required interest employees committee 84
21 since records process services attached personnel questions 96

22 manager possible insurance available department information 108
23 quality received necessary agreement additional development 120
24 reports contract education regarding management corporation 132

133 SENTENCES

These sentences can be used for 30-second and 1-minute "OK" timings.

25 The audit report concerning the federal research is needed. 12
26 The new procedure questions the monthly hospital inventory. 12 24
27 The new employee has recent experience operating computers. 12 36

28 My report requests a complete study of our telephone usage. 12 48
29 The members of the council approved the proposed purchases. 12 60
30 My customers question our business operations and products. 12 72

| 1 | 2 | 3 | 4 | 5 | 6 | 7 | 8 | 9 | 10 | 11 | 12

30 THE LETTER I

49   kik iii kik iii kIk IkI iIi IiI kik kkk kit kin Kim Kip iii   12

50   midi ibis digit civil ignite impish idolize imagine silicon   24
51   iris Iasi ivied mimic indict infirm inflict initial incline   36

52   ilium licit inlaid inkling digitizer auxiliary minicomputer   48

53   Iris is impartial in inflicting lucid limits on impish Kim.   12
54   Indian prints illustrate illustrious ingenuity in Illinois.   12

31 THE LETTER J

55   jjj jkj jjj jlj jjj j;j juj jyj jmj jnj jhj jjj Jim Joy jjj   12

56   jeer juju jerky jewel jujube jacket janitor jealous jetport   24
57   jamb jars jaunt jaded jejune jogged jesters jewelry jobless   36

58   jargon jonquil journal jeopardy jauntily judgment junctions   48

59   Joyful Jojo enjoys jangling junk jewelry and Japanese jade.   12
60   The jobless janitor was jealous of the jeweled judo jacket.   12

32 THE LETTER K

61   kkk kjk kkk klk kkk k;k kik k,k kkk kKk KkK Kik Kak Kol kkk   12

62   kick kink knock khaki kicker kicked kinfolk knuckle keynote   24
63   kyak kook kicky kapok knocks kopeck kickoff kitchen kidnaps   36

64   Kokomo kinship kidskin knickers knockout kickback knapsacks   48

65   Keli Kim kindly knits khaki knickers for kindergarten kids.   12
66   Keith and Karrie kept knives and kerosene from their kayak.   12

| 1 | 2 | 3 | 4 | 5 | 6 | 7 | 8 | 9 | 10 | 11 | 12

D<u>RILL</u>S

These vocabulary words occur so frequently in everyday written business communications that mastering them through drill will be of great benefit.

132 WORDS

Set a brisk pace on short words; maintain the pace on longer words.

For the swiftest gains in speed, repeat individual lines; but for greater gains in accuracy, repeat lines in groups as though they were three-line paragraphs.

1	of to in be is on we as by or at it an if no he us do me up	12
2	the and for you are our not all has any was can may new one	24
3	but his use who out had per its now day due see way job her	36
4	how pay tax set get she end did law air let off him gas act	48
5	that this will with have your from also time been year were	60
6	they work such each some more made when than cost only date	72
7	area plan must make very used them copy call city know what	84
8	need well like data form most would which these other their	96
9	into part over upon both same their shall order under about	108
10	last many rate then line days first after total state being	120
11	good next costs thank center before between special program	132
12	week feel years board should please company service meeting	144
13	help full above could office system project provide general	156

| 1 | 2 | 3 | 4 | 5 | 6 | 7 | 8 | 9 | 10 | 11 | 12 |

33 THE LETTER L

67 lll ljl lll lkl lll l;l lol l.l lll lLl LlL Lon Lin Lan lll   12

68 ball well skill label recall limply lawless loyally polling   24
69 tall fall llama lowly pillow lately likable liberal levelly   36

70 call lily parallel Hollerith satellite collection scrolling   48

71 Loyal Elli calls while lucky Lucille languishes listlessly.   12
72 Excellent local illustrators exhibit brilliant gallery art.   12

34 THE LETTER M

73 jmj mmm jmj mmm jMj MjM mMm MmM jmj mmm mom mum Mem Mam mmm   12

74 mums moms micro mommy moment mammal memoirs macrame summary   24
75 maim memo mummy mimic member marmot mammoth maximum minimum   36

76 Emma Mimi madam Sammy hammered commerce commands programmer   48

77 Momma and Mamie summoned Max to mark maximums and minimums.   12
78 My programmer must maintain commands for the microcomputer.   12

35 THE LETTER N

79 jnj nnn jnj nnn jNj NjN nNn NnN jnj nnn nun non Ned Nic nnn   12

80 neon none nanny annoy nankin nuance nonagon nunnery running   24
81 noon noun ninth inane cannot dinner oneness channel winning   36

82 none ninny scanner nonentity notation nonchalant nanosecond   48

83 Nineteen of the news media nominated my winning Nighthawks.   12
84 A funny nonunion nanny sunned newborn Nancy in the nursery.   12

| 1 | 2 | 3 | 4 | 5 | 6 | 7 | 8 | 9 | 10 | 11 | 12

37 ist enlist resist persist pianist soloist vocalist panelist   12

38 ity parity rarity utility quality ability futility futurity   24

39 ous mucous joyous envious anxious curious generous cautious   36

40 tor doctor factor realtor tractor auditor inventor detector   12   48

41 ure mature future pasture fixture torture fracture immature   24   60

42 ver sliver quiver cleaver whoever forever whatever whenever   36   72

43 able likable payable durable adaptable advisable profitable   12   84

44 ible audible visible legible invisible divisible reversible   24   96

45 tion diction portion mention exception education opposition   36 108

131 TWO-HAND
ALTERNATES

Speed up on these drills. The words are rhythmic and short. The two-letter, alternate-hand combinations are easy to type.

46 co come coat coin coco cone comb comic color comet coast co   12

47 fo form foot food fond foul foil focus folks focal force fo   24

48 he hear help heal head heel heap heavy heart heath hedge he   36

49 la late lady last lame lazy land large latch later labor la   12   48

50 le lean leaf lead left levy leap learn legal least leave le   24   60

51 ma made main make math mark mart maple match mayor manor ma   36   72

52 sp spat span spar spin spry spot spoil sport spent spell sp   12   84

53 th they them this then that than there think thing thick th   24   96

54 wh what whom when whiz whim whip while whale where wheel wh   36 108

| 1 | 2 | 3 | 4 | 5 | 6 | 7 | 8 | 9 | 10 | 11 | 12

36 THE LETTER O

85 lol ooo lol ooo lOl OlO oOo OoO lol ooo oak oil Ole Oka ooo   12

86 oboe oozy oomph robot oblong oolong outdoor obvious offload   24
87 loop book outdo outgo oology oodles outlook onerous opinion   36

88 odorous overload operator obnoxious opposition obsolescence   48

89 Oodles of odious orioles outfoxed oncoming odorous ocelots.   12
90 Otto obviously looks cooler on an outdoor oilcloth ottoman.   12

37 THE LETTER P

91 ;p; ppp ;p; ppp ;P; P;P pPp PpP ;p; ppp pop pep Pat Pam ppp   12

92 pomp papa papal pipit pipped popper panpipe paprika perplex   24
93 prep pump primp papaw pippin prepay pompous propped purpose   36

94 prompt floppy pineapple peripherals application Philippines   48

95 Pompous popular participants applauded peppy plump puppies.   12
96 Perceptive proprietors shipped purple papaya and pineapple.   12

38 THE LETTER Q

97 aqa qqq aqa qqq aQa QaQ qQq QqQ aqa qqq qua que Qui Quo qqq   12

98 quad quit queue quota quartz quasar qualify quantum quibble   24
99 quiz aqua quire query quiche equity quality inquiry squeeze   36

100 quadrant qualified quarterly equipment quiescent sequential   48

101 Qualified quarterbacks quickly quivered quality quadriceps.   12
102 Quite a quantity of quail and squab squash to quick quiche.   12

| 1 | 2 | 3 | 4 | 5 | 6 | 7 | 8 | 9 | 10 | 11 | 12

19 off office offend offense offhand officer offering official 12

20 per permit perish perjury perform percent perceive personal 24

21 pro profit proper profess process problem probably proceeds 36

22 rec record recede recline recover recount recourse receiver 12 48

23 sub subdue submit subject subsidy subside sublease subtract 24 60

24 the theory theirs therapy theater thermal theorems theorize 36 72

**130 WORD
ENDINGS**

These drills are good
for 1-minute timings
in which you learn to
hold your speed on
long-word copy.

25 age manage damage bandage baggage mileage coverage mortgage 12

26 ble usable bubble trouble visible taxable mailable sensible 24

27 ent parent accent dissent descent lenient adjacent resident 36

28 ess duress stress express empress regress needless progress 12 48

29 est invest attest dearest nearest longest shortest interest 24 60

30 ful cupful useful mindful helpful bashful grateful boastful 36 72

31 ial social serial special initial cordial material official 12 84

32 ify modify notify specify rectify glorify beautify simplify 24 96

33 ily bodily family happily moodily merrily mightily speedily 36 108

34 ing seeing asking telling singing begging thinking speaking 12 120

35 ion ration notion mention portion pension function junction 24 132

36 ise advise devise promise premise concise surprise exercise 36 144

| 1 | 2 | 3 | 4 | 5 | 6 | 7 | 8 | 9 | 10 | 11 | 12

39 THE LETTER R

103	frf rrr frf rrr fRf RfR rRr RrR frf rrr rag ran Ray Red rrr	12
104	rare purr rerun worry terror record arrange carrier warrant	24
105	roar curr rumor berry horror orator arrears barrier restore	36
106	overruns ferrous preferred recurrent irregular retrorockets	48
107	Ranchers or rustlers recovered a rare rattler in a rattrap.	12
108	Regular ferry river racers preferred irregular raspberries.	12

40 THE LETTER S

109	sss sas sss sds sss sfs sws sxs sss sSs SsS Sas Sis Sad sss	12
110	sass boss swiss ships stress kisses sassily success scissor	24
111	says bass sassy shoes misses sepsis glasses classes sisters	36
112	issue guesses systems classify embossed addresses processes	48
113	Shameless Suzi sidesteps salespersons to sip sassafras tea.	12
114	Sarcastic schoolmistresses suppress senseless sassy misses.	12

41 THE LETTER T

115	ftf ttt ftf ttt fTf TfT tTt TtT ftf ttt tag tar Ted Tod ttt	12
116	taut tilt taste taunt tattle tattoo testate attract trotter	24
117	tort mitt tutor witty attest totter attempt texture toaster	36
118	text plotter diskettes throughput transistor teletypewriter	48
119	Talkative terrorists told trite tales to taciturn tourists.	12
120	The tutor told Tom to tilt the teakettle and taste the tea.	12

| 1 | 2 | 3 | 4 | 5 | 6 | 7 | 8 | 9 | 10 | 11 | 12 |

DRILLS

Certain two- and three-letter combinations—some easy, some awkward—occur so frequently that mastering them through drill will pay rich dividends in both speed and accuracy.

129 WORD BEGINNINGS

For swiftest gains in speed, repeat individual lines; but for greater gains in accuracy, repeat lines in groups as though they were three-line paragraphs.

1	ac acrid accept accede access accent accord account achieve								12
2	ad adapt advise advice admire admits adverb address advance								24
3	an anger answer anyone anchor animal anyway analyze anxious								36
4	ap apart appear apples appall append appeal apology apparel							12	48
5	be being behalf begins belong behold beside believe benefit							24	60
6	de defer defeat debate deceit decree decide defense details							36	72
7	em ember emblem embark emboss employ emerge embargo empathy							12	84
8	en enact enroll encode engine enlist entail enlarge enclose							24	96
9	ex exact excuse expect excess excite except example examine							36	108
10	fa favor father factor facing fairly fading faculty falling							12	120
11	im image impose import immune impart impact imagine immerse							24	132
12	in index incite indeed indict infirm insure interim inquiry							36	144
13	pa panic paddle paints pamper parcel pastel package pastime							12	156
14	re recap recall reform remark regret recede receive reviews							24	168
15	un under unable unbend unless unreal unpaid unaware unknown							36	180
16	com comedy common company commend comment complain complete							12	192
17	con concur confer concept confirm confide congress conflict							24	204
18	cou courts county council courses courage courtesy countess							36	216

| 1 | 2 | 3 | 4 | 5 | 6 | 7 | 8 | 9 | 10 | 11 | 12 |

42 THE LETTER U

121   juj uuu juj uuu jUj UjU uUu UuU juj uuu uni uno Urn Use uuu   12

122   urge user uncut undue unique unjust ukulele unequal unglued   24
123   undo unit usury usurp unused untrue unlucky unquote uncouth   36

124   umlaut output subroutine throughput ubiquitous unscrupulous   48

125   Unjust understudies unscrupulously undercut unlucky actors.   12
126   Unpopular ushers use unusual and useless unstrung ukuleles.   12

43 THE LETTER V

127   fvf vvv fvf vvv fVf VfV vVv VvV fvf vvv vie vow Via Van vvv   12

128   viva vase valve verve velvet vivify vividly revival volcano   24
129   vive veto visit varve volume vivers velvety vervain visible   36

130   vine vivace volvulus vivacity valvular vivacious vaudeville   48

131   Very vain Vivian gave Vaughn a violet vase and velvet vest.   12
132   Vivacious volunteers vividly vetoed the visible vaudeville.   12

44 THE LETTER W

133   sws www sws www sWs WsW wWw WwW sws www was wow Wes Wil www   12

134   whew want wafer wagon willow winnow waxwork awkward warrant   24
135   wage weak waist water window wigwam wayward waxwing welfare   36

136   wallow worldwide whitewash waterworks wholewheat worthwhile   48

137   Walter wanted worthwhile Wedgwood and whitewashed woodwork.   12
138   Wayward Willy waged a winning war on waterweeds with Wally.   12

   | 1 | 2 | 3 | 4 | 5 | 6 | 7 | 8 | 9 | 10 | 11 | 12

ALTERNATE-RHYTHM WORDS

Maintain a steady, even pace on these words of varied length.

1	to the of the is the by the if the or the so the to the and	12
2	for an for me for it or go for he for us for of for the she	24
3	so risk so turn so wish so half so then so paid so work may	12
4	to bowl to both to form to hand to name to soak to wish pay	24
5	to amend to their to laugh to spend to field to focus right	12
6	by goals by rocks by dials by eight by forms by firms giant	24
7	aid fork air form rid land bog down big city end fish shape	12
8	did clan fix keys for maps apt goal cut cork and name whale	24
9	ant sign oak burn ape wish own oboe eye land sir dial sighs	36
10	due melt end auto spa bowl pay soak sit when big work girls	12
11	vow roam bus them key turn bid bush jay also may envy wicks	24
12	dye rich map pays got such row duty but paid box dock field	36
13	and signs the turns for risks the panel aid towns pay goals	12
14	for handy and firms big visit did blame fit their may title	24
15	with ivory when usual half signs idle audit than theme they	12
16	make turns wish vigor busy blame paid panel then laugh duty	24

Posttest

Repeat the 3-minute Pretest on page 61.

| 1 | 2 | 3 | 4 | 5 | 6 | 7 | 8 | 9 | 10 | 11 | 12

45 | THE LETTER X

139   sxs xxx sxs xxx sXs XsX xXx XxX sxs xxx xsw xas Xws Xwa xxx   12

140   exam oxen excel sixth excess sextet exclude sixteen execute   24
141   onyx axis xenon relax exceed reflex example excerpt extreme   36

142   xebec Xerox matrix exquisite xylophone executrix exaggerate   48

143   The excellent executrix exposed and examined the xylophone.   12
144   The excavator exerted much expertise and expanded the exit.   12

46 | THE LETTER Y

145   jyj yyy jyj yyy jYj YjY yYy YyY jyj yyy yam yet Ray May yyy   12

146   yard year yacht young yeasty yippie yardage yellowy tyrants   24
147   yarn easy yearn yummy yonder yearly yardarm loyalty pyramid   36

148   yen yolk yardage yachting youngberry yesteryear Yellowstone   48

149   Gary Kay and Ray Youngberry yearned to yacht at busy Yalta.   12
150   Say Jay may buy Gay yellow yarn yardage yearly in Yosemite.   12

47 | THE LETTER Z

151   aza zzz aza zzz aZa ZaZ zZz ZzZ aza zzz zoo zap Zip Zeb zzz   12

152   zero fuzz zebra fuzzy zipper dazzle zillion grizzly zealous   24
153   zeal jazz zilch frizz zigzag snazzy zoology swizzle frazzle   36

154   pizza drizzle pizzazz zestful zucchini stargazer razzmatazz   48

155   Zillions of snazzy czars swizzled and guzzled fuzzy fizzes.   12
156   Zany Zeb and crazy Zeke dazzled grizzly zebras in Zanzibar.   12

Posttest   Repeat the 3-minute Pretest on pages 10–11.

| 1 | 2 | 3 | 4 | 5 | 6 | 7 | 8 | 9 | 10 | 11 | 12

125 DOWNHILL WORDS

1	neighbor ancient emblems orient eighth proxy fight dial bid	12
2	problems penalty surname laughs island chair field burn did	24
3	mementos auditor socials formal dismay blend civic city got	36
4	quantity element ancient profit chapel blame giant than but	12
5	neuritis problem antique handle eighty handy shape work bus	24
6	downtown bicycle element bushel profit slang tight cork vow	36

126 ALTERNATE-HAND PHRASES

The vertical lines mark off the phrases; do not type or pause at the lines.

7	to me|it is|of it|to the|and may|of them|for them|with them	12
8	to us|to go|of us|by the|and the|by them|pay them|they work	24
9	to it|to do|by us|if the|and did|to wish|and them|with both	36
10	he is|if he|to it|is the|for the|is also|did make|they make	12
11	by it|if it|or if|do the|and got|is that|may make|when they	24
12	is to|do so|is he|so for|and for|to make|and they|they wish	36

127 ALTERNATE-HAND NAMES

13	for Blanche|and Vivian|for Durham|and Henry|to Blair|or Bob	12
14	for Claudia|and Rodney|for Buckey|and Clair|to Duane|or Sue	24
15	for England|and Dudley|for Helena|and Doris|to Burma|or Jay	36

\| 1 \| 2 \| 3 \| 4 \| 5 \| 6 \| 7 \| 8 \| 9 \| 10 \| 11 \| 12

ACCURACY AND CONCENTRATION

DRILLS

48 TRANS-POSITION ERRORS

When typing the following drills, use good technique, pay strict attention to the copy, and if necessary, type slowly—letter by letter.

ew	1	crew	blew	chews	renew	shrewd	nephew	dewdrop	viewing	stewing	12
we	2	weep	were	swept	weary	weekly	flower	showers	allowed	welcome	24
ie	3	diet	lien	yield	thief	friend	belief	believe	relieve	anxiety	36
ei	4	heir	vein	their	eight	sleigh	either	leisure	foreign	neither	48
oi	5	boil	void	avoid	point	adjoin	choice	appoint	jointly	hoisted	60
io	6	trio	lion	radio	riots	lotion	notion	opinion	caption	tension	72
op	7	open	hoop	opera	shops	proper	people	operate	dropped	opinion	84
po	8	port	upon	spots	poets	posted	polite	posture	portion	pollute	96
re	9	acre	rent	chore	agree	credit	parent	reasons	records	retreat	108
er	10	deer	ever	baker	order	barber	misery	battery	average	players	120

49 ADJACENT-KEY ERRORS

as	11	vase	rash	ashes	basic	master	washed	bananas	rascals	tastily	12
sa	12	saga	visa	saves	sauna	salary	safety	sailors	savages	satisfy	24
rt	13	sort	arts	apart	north	shirts	hearts	airport	resorts	shortly	36
tr	14	trot	tree	trays	trims	travel	street	treason	traffic	tractor	48
ui	15	quiz	ruin	fruit	suits	fluids	suites	cruises	bruises	guiding	60
ds	16	adds	beds	bands	beads	fields	scolds	affords	attends	spreads	72

| 1 | 2 | 3 | 4 | 5 | 6 | 7 | 8 | 9 | 10 | 11 | 12 |

These drills, in which the letters come from opposite sides of the keyboard, are fine for boosting speed.

122 ALTERNATE-HAND 3-LETTER WORDS

1 woe aid fur bus rid fox via oak may dug bow pay man dig box 12
2 key cod the men bit and rub wit but she bye fir owl sod tow 24
3 jam and cut for pen dog spa apt due urn sit bud rob own did 36

4 got air end lay big toe six cow foe eye dye fit bid pep sir 48
5 icy fix tie map hay Tod Sue Rod Bob Jay Kay Jan Ken Vic Leo 60

123 ALTERNATE-HAND 4-LETTER WORDS

6 firm idle maid hair both work half snow lend paid form rush 12
7 kept land when girl pens flap rich sick goal they worn lake 24
8 lame sock burn wish keys torn soak laid city down mend risk 36

9 owns fuel tidy sign lens turn rock them held pair soap town 48
10 such halt make foam Kent Glen Jake Clay Toby Ryan Dick Andy 60

124 ALTERNATE-HAND 5-LETTER WORDS

11 eight blame signs proxy vivid rigid cubic lapel field blend 12
12 theme right ivory their amend giant fight title burns handy 24
13 cycle shape whale vigor spend bland girls world shelf rocks 36

14 panel angle works focus goals chair usual laugh firms visit 48
15 audit civic dials Sybil Nancy Burke Chris Diana Cyrus Blake 60

| 1 | 2 | 3 | 4 | 5 | 6 | 7 | 8 | 9 | 10 | 11 | 12

e for i	17	idol into civic limit infirm hiring invalid inflict billing	12
i for e	18	ever seen earns three freeze events engrave decrees escapes	24
h for g	19	eggs gage aging gorge grudge rigged baggage suggest luggage	36
g for h	20	hush hash hatch which though highly rhythms highest harshly	48
y for t	21	tact test truth title totals letter attempt attains fitting	60
t for y	22	your jury mayor shyly yearly typing loyalty synonym younger	72
d for k	23	kick kirk khaki kapok kayaks knocks kicking knuckle kinfolk	84
k for d	24	deed adds dried ended middle indeed ladders bidders depends	96
r for u	25	unit undo usual undue unused useful unusual mutuals uncouth	108
u for r	26	roar rare error prior repair refers arrange carrier orderly	120

51 **SAME-FINGER ERRORS**

m for n	27	nine noun annex union annual cannot nunnery connect canning	12
n for m	28	memo mums maxim comma member commit immense mammoth summons	24
v for b	29	bomb bulb lobby hobby ribbon bubble nibbles babbles hobbies	36
b for v	30	view very vivid verve valves vastly revival vividly visited	48

52 **READING ERRORS**

Do not read ahead.
Keep eyes and
fingers together.

31	that than then maid mail male deal dear deer read reap reek	12
32	sale sage saga wear weak week talk tank take load loaf loft	24
33	need shed sled holy oily only bang long lung edge urge rage	36
34	list mist most make wake woke blab slab stab code mode made	48

| 1 | 2 | 3 | 4 | 5 | 6 | 7 | 8 | 9 | 10 | 11 | 12 |

ALTERNATE-RHYTHM SENTENCES

Boost speed by means of a series of 12-second timings. Then hold the rate for 30 seconds.

1 Ryan got both the land and lake and paid for half the dock. 12

2 They own dogs and paid the chap for pans for both the pens. 24

3 Toby and Glen got half the fish and hams for Jane and Suzi. 36

4 They may make the rich and busy bus firm fix both the maps. 12 48

5 Jane and Maud got half the duck and corn for Dick and Alan. 24 60

6 Both the city and town may make the chap fix both oak pens. 36 72

7 They pay Ryan and Jane for soap and keys and both big maps. 12 84

8 They may rush and soak the fish and yams for Alan and Ryan. 24 96

9 Ruby and Maud own both the cows and hens but wish for land. 36 108

10 Alan Dix paid for half the duck and also for corn and hams. 12 120

11 Ryan got both the maps and land and paid for half the bowl. 24 132

12 They got paid for corn and fish but wish for clay for Dick. 36 144

13 They got Glen and Ruby and Jake the land for fish and fowl. 12 156

14 Andy got both the oboe and auto and paid for half the cork. 24 168

15 Dick and Toby got busy and paid the city for both the keys. 36 180

| 1 | 2 | 3 | 4 | 5 | 6 | 7 | 8 | 9 | 10 | 11 | 12

53 PROXIMATE REACHES

```
aw  35  awful straw awning awhile awakens awkward awarding flawless   12
ax  36  axles taxis axioms taxing maximum coaxing relaxing axletree   24
dr  37  drive dream dragon dreary drawing drapery dressing dreadful   36

fe  38  ferns cafes fences safety fending feuding feelings feasible   48
hi  39  hives chide hinted hiring thinner hiccups shipping chickens   60
il  40  until wills skills filled thrills illegal illusion pilgrims   72

li  41  lists clips limits pliers sliding glimmer slippers reliable   84
nk  42  ankle trunk thinks monkey bankers ranking sinkable flunking   96
pl  43  plans plush plenty plural plywood plunged plumbing multiply  108

sc  44  discs scold school scheme screams scholar scribble scissors  120
se  45  seems sense series search sending seeking serenity severest  132
wa  46  water swaps washed walnut swallow wanting swapping swayback  144
```

54 LONG WORDS FOR CONCENTRATION

Type carefully.

```
47  business computer necessity arbitrary electronic collateral   12
48  absences definite conscious committee experience appreciate   24

49  boundary campaign emphasize negotiate thoroughly government   36
50  bankrupt amortize privilege occasions innovation skillfully   48

51  parallel omission sincerely warehouse summarized fascinated   60
52  misspell mortgage guarantee persuaded descendant continuous   72
```

```
|  1  |  2  |  3  |  4  |  5  |  6  |  7  |  8  |  9  |  10  |  11  |  12
```

ALTERNATE-HAND SENTENCES (Continued)

16 An idle neighbor may work to pay for the title to the auto. 12

17 The goal of Jane and Maud is to pay for the ham and turkey. 24

18 The sign is a visual aid for the antique bicycle and autos. 36

19 I am to go to work for the audit firm by the eighth of May. 12 48

20 The girl may wish to go to town to sign the proxy for them. 24 60

21 The rich widow may profit with a land firm by Lake Durhams. 36 72

22 Doris Rodney may sign the title for the giant cycle by May. 12 84

23 A penalty for the giant fight may end the work of the girl. 24 96

24 The city may fight to suspend the work of the downtown bus. 36 108

25 The sign of the authentic antique is the formal oak emblem. 12 120

26 The proficient city auditor may bid for handy ivory panels. 24 132

27 The civic visitor may pay for six or eight formal mementos. 36 144

28 Laurie and Rodney may lend their ancient and giant bicycle. 12 156

29 Chris did cut the eye a bit and may go to the city for aid. 24 168

30 The six forms she got for the firms may do for the problem. 36 180

| 1 | 2 | 3 | 4 | 5 | 6 | 7 | 8 | 9 | 10 | 11 | 12

NUMERIC LOCATIONAL SECURITY

DRILLS

Pretest/
Posttest

Take two 1-minute Pretests on each of the following paragraphs. Record the more accurate timing from each paragraph. After completing the drill work on the entire number section (pages 30–38), repeat these paragraphs as your Posttest.

55 STRAIGHT COPY

```
        The impact of the computer on our daily activities has    12
become greater and greater in the last few years.  The com-        24
puter is used in homes, businesses, and schools in hundreds        36
of different ways.  Computers come in all sizes and prices.        48
Many families have found the computer to be a valuable aid.        60
```

56 STRAIGHT COPY WITH NUMBERS

```
        In less than 50 years the computer industry has become     12
a $40 billion business for no less than 3,000 concerns.  In        24
1946 the first electronic digital computer was built.  With        36
18,000 vacuum tubes, it could multiply 2 numbers in about 3        48
milliseconds.  It had many wires and almost 7,000 switches.        60
```

57 DIGIT INVENTORY

```
8301 4902 6803 7904 4705 3406 5207 8608 9209 2510 3611 7512    12
5013 3414 5715 6816 7017 6318 4019 7520 8921 2822 9923 6324    24
1025 4926 7527 7628 4729 4230 9031 5732 1833 2034 9135 8636    36
3237 5038 8639 9740 2141 5542 1943 3644 6845 8146 2047 9048    48
7649 6250 2751 9352 8853 7054 2355 9056 3057 8958 1459 1160    60
```

```
|  1  |  2  |  3  |  4  |  5  |  6  |  7  |  8  |  9  |  10  |  11  |  12
```

120 ALTERNATE-HAND SENTENCES

These sentences are ideal for 1-minute and 30-second "OK" timings.

"OK" timings: Must be errorless for 30 seconds; not more than 1 error on 1-minute timings.

1 If they handle the formal city audit, it may end the fight. 12

2 Henry and Jan paid Helen for the land she owns by the lake. 24

3 The eight chaps may go right to the field with Bob and Tod. 36

4 Henry is busy with the work but may go to Lake City for us. 12 48

5 Diana did go to town with vigor to do the usual civic duty. 24 60

6 Doris or Andy may wish to go to work for the downtown firm. 36 72

7 He is busy with the air show for the Oak Lake civic social. 12 84

8 Pamela Bowman may wish to pay the neighbor for the bicycle. 24 96

9 A neighbor with neuritis problems may visit Zurich for aid. 36 108

10 They wish to blame the city firm for their big dog problem. 12 120

11 Dick may wish to work for an amendment for the civic panel. 24 132

12 Blanche Burman owns an auto and bicycle firm by Lake Irish. 36 144

13 The theme panel may fight for the title to the antique bus. 12 156

14 Rodney got title to half the land and half of Lake Orlando. 24 168

15 It is the duty of this panel to bid for eighty giant signs. 36 180

| 1 | 2 | 3 | 4 | 5 | 6 | 7 | 8 | 9 | 10 | 11 | 12

Practice

The only way to master number keys is to drill and drill. Force yourself to keep your eyes on the copy. Use the correct fingers and proper technique.

58 NUMBER KEYS 1–5

Use the 1 key on the top row. The 1 key *must* be used on computers.

Use the last sentence in each group for a Pretest/Posttest.

1   aaa aqa aaa ala ala aaa ala ala all all ala all all lal ala   12

2   aqqa alla alla alal alal alla lala llal llal alla alal llal   24

3   The 11 men ran 11 miles 11 times in 11 events for 111 days.   36

4   The 111 saved 11 size 11 items for 11 friends going May 11.   12 48

5   sss sws sss s2s s2s sss s2s s2s s22 s22 s2s s22 s22 2s2 s2s   12

6   swws s22s s22s s2s2 s2s2 s22s 2s2s 22s2 22s2 s22s s2s2 22s2   24

7   s2s 122 221 121 The 22 bought 12 items 21 times at gate 22.   36

8   We know 122 orders were shipped to 22 stores in 212 trucks.   12 48

9   ddd ded ddd d3d d3d ddd d3d d3d d33 d33 d3d d33 d33 3d3 d3d   12

10   deed d33d d33d d3d3 d3d3 d33d 3d3d 33d3 33d3 d33d d3d3 33d3   24

11   ded 133 331 131 We put 313 items on 31 tables for 13 hours.   36

12   Please sell my 333 tickets for the 13 plays within 31 days.   12 48

13   fff frf fff f4f f4f fff f4f f4f f44 f44 f4f f44 f44 4f4 f4f   12

14   frrf f44f f44f f4f4 f4f4 f44f 4f4f 44f4 44f4 f44f f4f4 44f4   24

15   f4f 144 441 141 Mail 4 stamps and 4 letters to the 41 boys.   36

16   Their 444 chickens ate the 41 sacks of food in only 4 days.   12 48

17   fff f5f fff f5f f5f fff f5f f5f f55 f55 f5f f55 f55 5f5 f5f   12

18   f55f f55f f55f f5f5 f5f5 f55f 5f5f 55f5 55f5 f55f f5f5 55f5   24

19   f5f 155 551 151 The 55 books are in 51 towns and 15 states.   36

20   She will collect 155 items to use in 515 ways for 5 months.   12 48

| 1 | 2 | 3 | 4 | 5 | 6 | 7 | 8 | 9 | 10 | 11 | 12

**Pretest/
Posttest**

Take two 3-minute Pretests on the following sentences. Record the more accurate of the two timings. After completing the drill work on this entire section (pages 62–67), repeat these sentences as your Posttest.

**119 ALTERNATE-
HAND
SENTENCES**

1 He may wish to fix the formal oak chair and the ivory keys.   12
2 Nancy Alan may wish to visit the firm with Helena and Kent.   24
3 The theme for the eighth panel is a big problem for Vivian.   36

4 Alan may pay for the signs and risk a fight with Henry Tod. 12 48
5 Claudia may go to work for the auditor to pay for the auto. 24 60
6 Helene Ryan paid for half of the ivory and half the enamel. 36 72

7 Six of the eight firms make a profit if they amend the bid. 12 84
8 He may take the big boat to the lake for Blanche and Cyrus. 24 96
9 Dick works for the city, but he may wish to work for Nancy. 36 108

10 Helen Dudley may rush to the city to sign the formal audit. 12 120
11 The firms may turn a big profit if they work with the city. 24 132
12 Dismal profits may make Jane Ryen suspend work by the lake. 36 144

13 If the men do their work by six, they may go to the social. 12 156
14 Ryan Burke may wish to rid the town of eighty dismal signs. 24 168
15 Eighty bushels of corn did make a tidy profit for Ruby Kay. 36 180

  | 1 | 2 | 3 | 4 | 5 | 6 | 7 | 8 | 9 | 10 | 11 | 12

21	jjj j6j jjj j6j j6j jjj j6j j6j j66 j66 j6j j66 j66 6j6 j6j	12
22	j66j j66j j66j j6j6 j6j6 j66j 6j6j 66j6 66j6 j66j j6j6 66j6	24
23	j6j 166 661 161 Send 66 people to do 61 sets for 161 shows.	36
24	The 166 men worked 61 hours in 16 inches of debris and mud.	12 48
25	jjj juj jjj j7j j7j jjj j7j j7j j77 j77 j7j j77 j77 7j7 j7j	12
26	juuj j77j j77j j7j7 j7j7 j77j 7j7j 77j7 77j7 j77j j7j7 77j7	24
27	j7j 177 771 171 Please buy 17 cups and 17 saucers by May 7.	36
28	I need 77 reams of bond within 17 days for 17 classes of 7.	12 48
29	kkk kik kkk k8k k8k kkk k8k k8k k88 k88 k8k k88 k88 8k8 k8k	12
30	kiik k88k k88k k8k8 k8k8 k88k 8k8k 88k8 88k8 k88k k8k8 88k8	24
31	k8k 188 881 181 My 18 years of teaching grade 8 end June 8.	36
32	She shipped 88 packages of 18 pounds 8 ounces to 81 cities.	12 48

Use the L key for the
9 reach.

Use the 1 key
starting here.

33	lll lol lll l9l l9l lll l9l l9l l99 l99 l9l l99 l99 9l9 l9l	12
34	lool l99l l99l l9l9 l9l9 l99l 9l9l 99l9 99l9 l99l l9l9 99l9	24
35	l9l l99 99l l9l The 19 test scores range between 91 and 99.	36
36	We announced 91 men and 99 women earned 919 points totally.	12 48
37	;;; ;p; ;;; ;0; ;0; ;;; ;0; ;0; ;00 ;00 ;0; ;00 ;00 0;0 ;0;	12
38	;pp; ;00; ;00; ;0;0 ;0;0 ;00; 0;0; 00;0 00;0 ;00; ;0;0 00;0	24
39	;0; 100 001 101 The 10 women drove 100 miles every 10 days.	36
40	The 101 applicants scored between 100 and 110 on 10 skills.	12 48

| 1 | 2 | 3 | 4 | 5 | 6 | 7 | 8 | 9 | 10 | 11 | 12

1   Once in a while I find myself thinking over the time I   12
lived in tiny midwestern towns. Rural living taught me how   24
much smiles or warm comments mean to friends and neighbors.   36

2   Summertime brought the circus and group sports such as   12   48
baseball and racing. Midafternoon meant long swims, diving   24   60
for coins, or racing up and down the area. The sun gave us   36   72
sunburn, while the steaming sidewalks burned our bare feet.   48   84

3   Winters brought an extremely severe climate with ample   12   96
snow and ice. Happy times abounded on ice skates. Snowmen   24   108
and snowballs began to overcome young minds. At night warm   36   120
and heavy blankets brought the very nice effect of a haven.   48   132

4   A trademark is often a picture, symbol, word, mark, or   12   144
figure used to make some product stand out from all others.   24   156
At first, pictures or symbols were used because most people   36   168
could not read or write. Do you recall the barber pole and   48   180
its red and white stripes? One really did not have to know   60   192
how to read to know its meaning. The pole served as a sign   72   204
of the fact that one seeking a barber would find one there.   84   216

Posttest   Repeat the 3-minute Pretest on page 55.

| 1 | 2 | 3 | 4 | 5 | 6 | 7 | 8 | 9 | 10 | 11 | 12

These sentences are ideal for 1-minute "OK" timings.

"OK" timings: Typing with no more than 1 error per minute.

1 The 11 men won 111 prizes in 11 games and 11 in 111 others. 12
2 He has seat 1 in car 1 of train 1, which is now at gate 11. 12 24

3 Send the 22 tablets, 22 pencils, 22 books, and 222 erasers. 12 36
4 Send 12 to us, 21 to John, 22 to Richard, and 211 to Grace. 12 48

5 She saw 33 towns, 31 villages, 313 cities, and 13 counties. 12 60
6 The hotel lost 31 sheets or towels in 3 months and 13 days. 12 72

7 The dates were May 14, 1414; May 4, 1441; and May 14, 1444. 12 84
8 The law was passed on June 14, 1441, not November 14, 1441. 12 96

9 It took 5 months, 5 weeks, 5 days, 5 hours, and 15 minutes. 12 108
10 He sold 115 in March, 151 in April, and 155 or more in May. 12 120

11 William has 6 brothers, 6 sisters, 16 uncles, and 16 aunts. 12 132
12 On January 16, 66 houses and 61 barns burned to the ground. 12 144

13 He has 177 pennies, 171 nickels, 77 dimes, and 71 quarters. 12 156
14 The 71 settlers and the 17 animals arrived here about 1771. 12 168

15 She has 8 hats, 18 skirts, 18 dresses, 8 suits, and 1 coat. 12 180
16 He bought 81 pounds of number 18 nails on October 18, 1881. 12 192

17 They sold him 9 chairs, 19 tables, 91 lamps, and 119 desks. 12 204
18 The new school holds 919 students; the older one, 991 more. 12 216

19 There are 1,010 creeks, 100 rivers, and 100 lakes up there. 12 228
20 They gave 1,001 persons 1,100 promissory notes in 100 days. 12 240

| 1 | 2 | 3 | 4 | 5 | 6 | 7 | 8 | 9 | 10 | 11 | 12

114 FIRST ROW UP TO HOME

Pretest   13   Cal lacks a small black bag and calls Val back at the bank.   12

Practice   14   van can bad bag ball bank band balk class calls basal banal   12
              15   bah cam cad ban bald clad call back blank balsa chalk black   24
              16   baa cab ban Mal calf vain base vase balls small cabal basks   36

Posttest   Repeat the Pretest.

115 FIRST ROW UP TO THIRD

Pretest   17   Cec may buy my boots to view the berry crops and the moors.   12

Practice   18   now vie cut vet more very zero core cramp vixen mixer merry   12
              19   bow cue not bit note mutt veer bout liver crane venom moors   24
              20   but may mop cry view boot crow crop berry berth amber Crete   36

Posttest   Repeat the Pretest.

116 THIRD ROW DOWN TO FIRST

Pretest   21   Yvonne won a prize urn from Mexico at that open town forum.   12

Practice   22   pun own urn rim open prom turn ruin forum toxin nouns round   12
              23   ton pin run tub town upon worm quiz perch prize queen preen   24
              24   yen rib yum one item iron poem punt yummy tumor bumpy zones   36

Posttest   Repeat the Pretest.

117 ONE-FINGER VERTICALS

25   br bro bran brag hu hug hut hub gr gri grow grub fr fro fry   12
26   ny any many zany nu nub nut nun rb orb barb herb mu mud mum   24

| 1 | 2 | 3 | 4 | 5 | 6 | 7 | 8 | 9 | 10 | 11 | 12

60 BASIC WE-23 DRILLS

These drills use the same fingers for the letters and the following number.

1	we 23 up 70 to 59 or 94 it 85 yo 69 et 35 io 89 ur 74 re 43								12
2	wee 233 you 697 wow 292 eye 363 rot 495 wry 246 yet 635 635								24
3	wet 235 pie 083 rip 480 pit 085 rut 475 pop 090 too 599 599								36
4	wey 236 put 075 rue 473 yee 633 woo 299 pup 070 wew 232 232								48
5	wit 285 ore 943 tut 575 our 974 yew 632 try 546 ire 843 843								60

61 CENTURY DRIVE

Goal: To reach 100 within 2 minutes.

For variety substitute the following words: *the, for, did, but.*

6 and 1 and 2 and 3 and 4 and 5 and 6 and 7 and 8 and 9 and 10
and 11 and 12 and 13 and 14 and 15 and 16 and 17 and 18 and 19
and 20 and 21 and 22 and 23 and 24 and 25 and 26 and 27 and 28
and 29 and 30 and 31 and 32 and 33 and 34 and 35 and 36 and 37
and 38 and 39 and 40 and 41 and 42 and 43 and 44 and 45 and 46
and 47 and 48 and 49 and 50 and 51 and 52 and 53 and 54 and 55
and 56 and 57 and 58 and 59 and 60 and 61 and 62 and 63 and 64
and 65 and 66 and 67 and 68 and 69 and 70 and 71 and 72 and 73
and 74 and 75 and 76 and 77 and 78 and 79 and 80 and 81 and 82
and 83 and 84 and 85 and 86 and 87 and 88 and 89 and 90 and 91
and 92 and 93 and 94 and 95 and 96 and 97 and 98 and 99 and 100

62 DIGIT INVENTORY

Goal: To type accurately and increase speed with each 1-minute timing.

7	6701 8202 6303 7204 8705 9606 2707 1008 7409 8510 9311 8212												12
	7613 6714 7015 6116 1017 5618 4919 3920 2821 1622 1723 1624												24
	9725 8626 6727 5028 4729 3930 2831 7632 6733 6534 7435 1036												36
	8737 1938 6739 9340 8241 7742 9843 9044 5645 4046 3947 2848												48
	8049 3850 4851 2852 9453 5954 8955 9356 9857 9958 9059 4860												60

| 1 | 2 | 3 | 4 | 5 | 6 | 7 | 8 | 9 | 10 | 11 | 12

Vertical Reaches

To minimize arm and hand motions, keep your wrists low and parallel and curve your fingers so that you can type on their tips. Take a 1-minute timing on the Pretest, practice the drill lines for 3 to 5 minutes, and then take the Posttest.

111 HOME ROW UP TO THIRD

Pretest	1	Pat Gray heard that the happy jury freed his little sister.	12
Practice	2	jut ode lay how deep lope free soft floor after offer jelly	12
	3	hip pat fly air fret ride drop kite delay sorry judge slyly	24
	4	his key par she fray jury kiss swap these ought dryly frame	36
Posttest		Repeat the Pretest.	

112 THIRD ROW DOWN TO HOME

Pretest	5	The usual quota for oil was equal to rates of rush periods.	12
Practice	6	rig owl wag ill rush pull yolk risk erred equal staff rates	12
	7	pal oil rid era wish pool owls talk quota youth toils yelps	24
	8	tug rag oak red yell peak pole rate usual pulls yells stays	36
Posttest		Repeat the Pretest.	

113 HOME ROW DOWN TO FIRST

Pretest	9	Jan Lanz can calmly scan axles as Allan lacks jacks to jam.	12
Practice	10	lax jab dab ham scan ajax calm land avast jambs lambs scabs	12
	11	jam adz sac nab slab lamb labs slam palms lacks sacks backs	24
	12	ban ack can lab alms jazz flax jamb axles laces jacks hacks	36
Posttest		Repeat the Pretest.	

| 1 | 2 | 3 | 4 | 5 | 6 | 7 | 8 | 9 | 10 | 11 | 12

63 NUMBER SENTENCES

These sentences are ideal for 1-minute and 30-second "OK" timings.

1 There were 739 tickets left for 34 shows to begin March 16.   12
2 Unit 21 has 95 suites with only 66 tenants using 19 floors.   24
3 I need 82 boxes to send to 34 states for 80 variety stores.   36
4 The 14 men and 25 women ran 6 miles, swam 10, and biked 17.   48

5 The clerks counted 245 books, 479 tablets, and 63 staplers.   12 60
6 Get 22 men to carry the 70 trunks left by the 159 students.   24 72
7 On January 16, 38 dogs and 20 cats were given to 15 people.   36 84
8 During March, 49 storms tossed 135 logs onto 68 new cabins.   48 96

9 The 26 instructors taught 747 pupils more than 15 subjects.   12 108
10 Our new band needs 19 drums, 18 clarinets, and 10 trumpets.   24 120
11 I must now hire 13 clerks, 6 stenos, and 8 word processors.   36 132
12 He visited 20 countries and 35 cities in less than 49 days.   48 144

13 We raised 22 ponies, 16 kittens, 8 puppies, and 6 chickens.   12 156
14 The big sale runs May 9, 10, and 11 in 53 different stores.   24 168
15 The big accident involved 10 trucks, 9 cars, and 47 people.   36 180
16 The bakery needed 450 sacks of flour for 730 dozen cookies.   48 192

17 More than 974 adults and 653 children will meet January 16.   12 204
18 There were 17 hydros in the August 8 race viewed by 99,870.   24 216
19 The 86 joggers waited 20 minutes before the crowd of 3,045.   36 228
20 The 4 women and 12 children each need 3 sets of 26 tickets.   48 240

| 1 | 2 | 3 | 4 | 5 | 6 | 7 | 8 | 9 | 10 | 11 | 12 |

108 THIRD ROW

Pretest

Practice
To make upward reaches, extend your fingers. Do not move your hands.

Posttest

13 She must try to write a clear report for the troop leaders. 12

14 aqaqa ;p;p; swsws lolol deded kikik frfrf jujuj ftftf jyjyj 12

15 out wet two pup were pipe port pore quire piper equip power 24

16 eye tip try owe tire trip quit quay write wrote quite quiet 36

17 our row you yet your true pert tout queue quoit troop tower 48

18 pop|too wet|you owe|our trip|try your|poor power|your troop 60

Repeat the Pretest.

109 IN-ROCKS

Pretest

Practice
Don't let your hands be pulled from position by in-motions such as "ag" and "pu."

Posttest

19 One agent agreed to apply most labor costs toward our boat. 12

20 wag won sag cat puff sort cart pest cough purse agree after 12

21 eat war put ate army pity purr cafe agent lunch labor costs 24

22 aft ago cab lug page once able boat spout dough coast water 36

23 ohm|one cat|won war|are able|one boat|army agent|most labor 48

Repeat the Pretest.

110 OUT-ROCKS

Pretest

Practice
Keep your arms and hands steady; let your fingers do all the work!

Posttest

24 Gayle will take short trips to the farm on the upper route. 12

25 tan now cup tax whip take tank game croup those short group 12

26 nor hoe van how nope tame yore fume quite whole upper young 24

27 mob bay mow not ripe gale trip dupe honor gaudy motor gaily 36

28 day|not now|tax ban|how ripe|tan tank|tame group|take trips 48

Repeat the Pretest.

| 1 | 2 | 3 | 4 | 5 | 6 | 7 | 8 | 9 | 10 | 11 | 12

Take 1-minute timings on all paragraphs. Try to maintain the speed you reached on the first paragraph when typing subsequent paragraphs.

1 4477 3388 2299 1100 5566 4477 3388 2299 1100 5566 4477 3388   12
   4747 3838 2929 1010 5656 4747 3838 2929 1010 5656 4747 3838   24
   4738 2910 5647 3829 1056 4738 2910 5647 3829 1056 4738 2910   36

2 2937 8410 5629 3648 5017 9261 4058 7302 1748 3659 1982 6534   12
   3679 2801 5349 1276 4508 7139 6542 8095 0673 1482 9120 4637   24
   1034 2915 3856 4762 5876 6589 7490 8371 4012 9207 2935 0413   36

3 2.6 0.1 8.5 4.3 7.0 6.1 8.8 9.4 2.0 3.2 7.4 1.5 9.9 7.3 5.6   12
   8.39 70.1 8.32 51.4 99.3 1.46 50.5 0.88 7.47 2.22 68.6 90.7   24
   7.428 39.10 559.6 2.888 41.36 607.7 5.112 43.34 92.57 900.6   36

4 4,300 6,271 9,855 1,095 2,349 7,862 1,467 3,854 9,701 2,638   12
   6,153 2,141 9,420 8,672 4,092 3,764 8,903 5,798 1,375 5,806   24
   9,026 4,785 2,039 6,140 1,936 6,574 2,843 5,170 3,788 5,219   36

5 $123 $907 $645 $832 $503 $481 $610 $954 $321 $879 $660 $579   12
   $2,998 $1,003 $6,681 $3,874 $4,552 $62,379 $52,130 $487,916   24
   $1.23 $46.75 $64.03 $100.93 $3,794.15 $88,916.02 $68,574.23   36

6 27% 46% 71% 98% 54% 32% 67% 52% 30% 83% 91% 10% 65% 80% 49%   12
   14.6% 8.87% 33.5% 1.92% 45.6% 8.12% 9.09% 20.7% 5.73% 60.4%   24
   26% 49.73% 50.12% 63.98% 100.2% 87.66% 52.43% 511.3% 87.94%   36

   | 1 | 2 | 3 | 4 | 5 | 6 | 7 | 8 | 9 | 10 | 11 | 12

Horizontal Reaches

For maximum value, position your body and hands as described on page 1. Take a 1-minute timing on the Pretest, practice the drill lines for 3 to 5 minutes, and then take the Posttest.

106 HOME ROW

Pretest

1 Ada had a fall and has had a lad add all dad's glass flags.   12

Practice
This is especially good for reducing hand bouncing and for helping you hold the home position.

2 sad gas lad ash fall sash adds alas halls glass salad sagas   12
3 has ask had lag half glad sass lash slash flags flash falls   24
4 fad gag jag dad gala dash flag saga shall flask slags Allan   36

5 sag|sad lad|dad has|ash fall|has hash|lass shall|glad sagas   48
6 ;';|add gas|ask all|had half|had lash|gala flags|Al's salad   60

Posttest

Repeat the Pretest.

107 BOTTOM ROW OF KEYS

Pretest

7 Von can box bibs and combs and bank a maximum sum of money.   12

Practice
To make downward strokes, curve your fingers and stab. Do not let your hands move.

8 azaza ;/;/; sxsxs l.l.l dcdcd k,k,k fvfvf jmjmj fbfbf jnjnj   12
9 box mix can nab numb buzz back name comma venom civic comic   24
10 van man bib mob zinc bomb comb lynx maxim annex zombi nanny   36

11 cab, ban, cob, mob, nob, men, box, can, mum, Nan, Ben, Van,   48
12 oz. a.m. p.m. c.o.d. f.o.b. cn/mb C/M V/N zinc? numb? comb?   60

Posttest

Repeat the Pretest.

| 1 | 2 | 3 | 4 | 5 | 6 | 7 | 8 | 9 | 10 | 11 | 12

Fairly easy copy.

Practice each paragraph before taking 3-minute timings on the whole page.

Average syllables per word: 1.32

Average figures per number: 3

1   Two members of the 1964 class of Blair High School are   12
chairing a group of 18 to look for a resort for the 20-year   24
class reunion. A lovely place 78 miles from the city turns   36
out to be the best. It has 254 rooms and a banquet hall to   48
seat 378. It has been open 365 days per year since opening   60
on May 30, 1926. They will need 450 to reserve the resort.   72

2   Debbie Holmes was put in charge of buying 2,847 office   12   84
machines for the entire firm. Debbie visited more than 109   24   96
companies in 35 states in 6 months. She will report to the   36 108
board today in Room 2784 at 5 p.m. The board will consider   48 120
her report about those 109 firms and recommend the top 2 or   60 132
3 brands to purchase. Debbie must decide before August 16.   72 144

3   Lynn Greene said work started on the project March 27,   12 156
1983. The 246 blueprints were mailed to the office 18 days   24 168
ago. The prints had to be 100 percent accurate before they   36 180
were acceptable. The project should be finished by May 31,   48 192
1985. At that time there will be 47 new condominiums, each   60 204
having at least 16 rooms. The building will be 25 stories.   72 216

| 1 | 2 | 3 | 4 | 5 | 6 | 7 | 8 | 9 | 10 | 11 | 12

HORIZONTAL- AND VERTICAL-REACH

DRILLS

Pretest/ Posttest

Take two 3-minute Pretests on the following paragraphs. Record the more accurate of the two timings. After completing the drill work on this section (pages 56–60), repeat these paragraphs as your Posttest.

105 HORIZONTAL/ VERTICAL PARAGRAPHS

1   From time to time I think of how things are now in our   12
town and remember how they were years ago. Rural residents   24
were noted for playing and working with very great jollity.   36
Happy youths talked and laughed when classes were dismissed   48
for the year. Annual summer trips offered many merry days.   60

2   During playtime in the summer each member of our group   12 72
was sure to be busy with some game or craft. Swimming plus   24 84
hiking and camping was great fun for all of us. Summertime   36 96
was a great time for skating and walking in the quiet park.   48 108
The end of summer brought rainy days and the big gala ball.   60 120

3   I happily remember our winter activities. After daily   12 132
lessons, we would dash back home and clean our rooms. Very   24 144
soon our group would meet at the plaza for making snowballs   36 156
and sledding. Each Sunday we met at the pond to ice skate.   48 168
All in all, many things really have not changed in my town.   60 180

| 1 | 2 | 3 | 4 | 5 | 6 | 7 | 8 | 9 | 10 | 11 | 12 |

Normal copy.

Practice each paragraph before taking 3-minute timings on the whole page.

Average syllables per word: 1.41

Average figures per number: 3

4   December 17, 1903, is the birth date of all airplanes.   12
Orville and Wilbur Wright started building gliders in 1900.   24
In 1903, they built a motor and propeller for their glider.   36
Orville made the first flight, which lasted 12 seconds, and   48
flew 120 feet. Wilbur's flight was 852 feet in 59 seconds.   60

5   These first flights in 1903 were just the start of the   12 72
evolution of planes. By the year 1909, Bleriot had crossed   24 84
the English Channel. By the year 1912, a two-piece plywood   36 96
fuselage was built for greater strength. By the 1930s, the   48 108
all-metal fuselage was tried, and it soon appeared in DC3s.   60 120

6   From the Wrights' 1903 motor and prop came the engines   12 132
for the 1950 turbojet that generated at least 19,600 pounds   24 144
of thrust. The big Boeing 747 has four engines with 50,000   36 156
pounds of thrust each. The future holds an advanced super-   48 168
sonic jet with a saving of almost 40 percent in fuel usage.   60 180

| 1 | 2 | 3 | 4 | 5 | 6 | 7 | 8 | 9 | 10 | 11 | 12

103 THIRD FINGER

Pretest 15 Vexed Wes assessed an excess of oil in my pool in Honolulu. 12

FOURTH FINGER

Pretest   16 A plump nippy puppy gazed as a crazed czar zagged in water. 12

Practice   17 weds lull razz pulp data polo area only sew ill saw lop zag 12
             18 dews loll bass pump west look stew poll wax oil was pop zax 24

             19 asset swab was holly pool lop sexes sets sax loony pomp pop 36
             20 abate saws Ada knoll loom Lon graze axes Wes jolly Pipi pup 48

             21 waxweeds Honolulu bazaar pompom Warsaw poplin Wes pip we up 60
             22 excesses lollipop excess Kokomo street pompon sex ill as pi 72

Posttest   Repeat the Pretests.

104 LEFT-HAND/ RIGHT-HAND SENTENCES

Use these sentences for 30-second and 1-minute timings.

23 You were in a great car in my garage on East Mullin Street.   12
24 Jill gave my dad a pumpkin after we agreed on a secret bet. 12   24
25 Jimmy Rex saw a devastated beggar in tattered taffeta rags. 12   36

26 You get a minimum trade rate on a seat on my fastest craft. 12   48
27 Phillip Reed creates excessive stress on my nonunion staff. 12   60
28 Only Rebecca was in grave arrears on my east acreage tract. 12   72

29 Carefree Philly ate my pink lollipop in Honolulu at Easter. 12   84
30 You gave Johnny an unholy scare after you drew a drab face. 12   96

Try this using the left hand only.

31 A secret war was aggravated as a dazed beggar was set free. 12 108

Posttest   Repeat the Pretest on page 48.

| 1 | 2 | 3 | 4 | 5 | 6 | 7 | 8 | 9 | 10 | 11 | 12

Fairly hard copy.

Practice each paragraph before taking 3-minute timings on the whole page.

Average syllables per word: 1.55

Average figures per number: 3

7   Income before securities transactions was up 10.8 per-   12
cent from $13.49 million in 1982 to $14.95 million in 1983.   24
Earnings per share (adjusted for a 10.5 percent stock divi-   36
dend distributed on August 26) advanced 10 percent to $2.39   48
in 1983 from $2.17 in 1982. Earnings may rise for 7 years.   60
Hopefully, earnings per share will grow another 10 percent.   72

8   Kosy, Klemin, and Bille began selling on May 23, 1964. 12 84
Their second store was founded in Renton on August 3, 1965. 24 96
From 1964 to 1984, they opened more than 50 stores through- 36 108
out the country. As they expanded, 12 regional offices had 48 120
to be organized. Each of these 12 regions employs from 108 60 132
to 578 people. National headquarters employs 1,077 people. 72 144

9   Carole owns 118 stores located in 75 cities ranging as 12 156
far west as Seattle and as far east as Boston. She owns 46 24 168
stores south of the Mason-Dixon line and 24 stores north of 36 180
Denver. Carole buys goods from 89 companies located in 123 48 192
countries and all 50 states. Carole started in business on 60 204
March 3, 1975. She had less than $6,000 in capital assets. 72 216

Posttest   Repeat the 1-minute Pretests on page 29.

| 1 | 2 | 3 | 4 | 5 | 6 | 7 | 8 | 9 | 10 | 11 | 12

Take a 1-minute timing on the Pretest. Practice the drill lines for 3 to 5 minutes. Then take the Posttest.

101 FIRST FINGER

Pretest	1	Gregg better barter for a minimum of hominy from my garage.	12
Practice	2	barters homonym tartar unholy graft jumpy garb noun err mum	12
	3	regrets minimum garage hominy refer mummy brag hump rat hum	24
	4	treat raft get lymph hymn joy egret brat bar unpin July inn	36
	5	verge verb art ninny puny nun tract fret tag yummy Lynn you	48
	6	beggars ferret grate grab bag minikin minion humpy mump mun	60
	7	taffeta better fever tart rag opinion phylon humph John him	72
Posttest		Repeat the Pretest.	

102 SECOND FINGER

Pretest	8	Dazed Kimmi and Eve dread severe tatters on my pink kimono.	12
Practice	9	geezers minikin career pipkin dread kinky seed kiln dad kin	12
	10	decreed million degree kimono deter milky deed mink cad ink	24
	11	creed edge fed Kikki link Mik greed deer add ilium kilo kip	36
	12	evade dead ace kinin ikon kin adder weed eve pinky kino Kim	48
	13	decades secede cease debt wed pinkily pipkin Pippi inky Nik	60
	14	decease secret geese beds see Phillip kimono Kinin kink ilk	72
Posttest		Repeat the Pretest.	

| 1 | 2 | 3 | 4 | 5 | 6 | 7 | 8 | 9 | 10 | 11 | 12 |

DOUBLE-LETTER

D<u>RILL</u>S

Take two 3-minute pretests on the following paragraphs. Record the more accurate of the two timings. After completing the drill work on this section (pages 40–42), repeat these paragraphs as your Posttest.

**68 DOUBLE-
LETTER
PARAGRAPHS**

Eighteen brilliant employees on their accounting staff	12
were annoyed by a puzzling dilemma. A cool million dollars	24
seemed to have disappeared. Apparently a terrible employee	36
was embezzling excess funds from three commercial accounts.	48
This issue was to affect the feeling of freedom in the main	60
office. Proof of illegal intent was essential. The doomed	72
accountants began to assess their worrisome loss of assets.	84
Success in solving the irregular riddle was soon to follow.	96
One embarrassed accountant had to confess to a loss of	108
glasses as well as inaccuracy in proofing. So arrangements	120
followed to correct the error. All this fuss happened when	132
a small comma became a bigger dot on the scribbled records.	144
Happily the boss could not now harass the very foolish	156
accountant for the accidental and obviously innocent error.	168
The gloom in the room fizzled as this muddle was forgotten.	180

| 1 | 2 | 3 | 4 | 5 | 6 | 7 | 8 | 9 | 10 | 11 | 12

97 FIRST FINGER

16 err rag tab vat bag rat tag bar aft gab raft tart barb garb   12

17 tar bat tat art far beg fat bet get ebb verb brag fret brat   24

18 barge great abaft greet staff avert beret graft treat tract 12 36

19 grave draft refer after verve egret verge craft grate fever 24 48

20 attest begged barter revert strata tartar affect garage Art 12 60

21 target barber garter tatter batter street dagger adverb Tab 24 72

22 beggar ferret garret better rafter regret teeter bearer Red 36 84

98 SECOND FINGER

23 ace dad add eve cad fed red bee wee bed fee see tee dew Deb 12 96

24 deer edge breed bedew cadet zebec cedar geese defeat facade 24 108

25 seed deed tweed freed wedge dazed dread deter effect secede 36 120

26 weed dead creed greed adder cease evade edged career degree 48 132

27 settee accede exceed freeze recede access excess wedded Cec 12 144

28 secret arcade create decade geezer decree crease severe Eve 24 156

99 THIRD FINGER

29 we sew wax sets bass stew dews saws Bess vexes brass stress 12 168

30 as saw was west swab weds sews axes Wess sweet asset excess 24 180

100 FOURTH FINGER

31 zag area data faze afar saga award abaft agate zebra strata 12 192

32 zax adze gaze raze czar razz dazed adage craze abate bazaar 24 204

| 1 | 2 | 3 | 4 | 5 | 6 | 7 | 8 | 9 | 10 | 11 | 12

Practice

The faster you type, the more troublesome double letters become. Learn to accent the second letter of the pair slightly.

69 **DOUBLES IN WORDS**

Set a brisk pace on short words; maintain the pace on longer words.

1	see egg too off zoo tool putt miss jazz full been burr mitt	12
2	boo ill bee ebb tee cuff book pass well soon muff bill zoom	24
3	add all odd err inn tall less buzz pool seem ooze boss buff	36
4	toss knee book fluff dizzy funny skill brooks bigger errors	48
5	mill feel hood added goods small seeks differ fillet common	60
6	fool will cool class proof green comma happen little smooth	72
7	need ball food breed flood drill putty robber letter snooze	84
8	good fill feel cliff witty asset seeks accord keeper summer	96
9	keep wall look hilly guess abbey rummy begged cannot bottle	108
10	doll sees tummy apple accept supper blabber shopper loggers	120
11	door loll ditto gummy jobber agreed tariffs cutting getting	132
12	mess took petty sleep rubber gummed between express million	144

70 **ALPHABETIC DOUBLES**

13	bb ribbon bubbles cabbage bobbing hobbies cobblers scribble	12
14	cc occupy accused account succeed acclaim accident occasion	24
15	dd middle fiddler ladders maddest muddled addition suddenly	36
16	ee esteem deepest feeding misdeed fifteen employee disagree	48
17	ff muffle differs effects chiffon efforts affluent sufferer	60
18	gg dagger suggest baggage beggars digging druggist bragging	72

| 1 | 2 | 3 | 4 | 5 | 6 | 7 | 8 | 9 | 10 | 11 | 12 |

LEFT-HAND WORDS

Keep both hands in the proper typing position.

1   at ax ba fa age bat cab dad ear fat gas rag sat tag vat was   12

2   as ad be we ate bad cat dab eat far get red sea tea vet wet   24

3   area brag care date ever fast garb rage sage tear vase were   12   36

4   aged bear crab dear ease fear gave scab rear test veer ware   24   48

5   awed best crew drab eggs feat gaze read seat text vest weed   36   60

6   acts brew czar debt erst fate grab rare stew tare ward wade   48   72

7   aware baste cedar draft farce grate serve treat waste xebec   12   84

8   asset beard crate eager fever react stage verse weave zebra   24   96

9   adage brave defer evade graze radar taste verge cease zebec   36   108

10   adverb desert garbage steward weavers beverage deceased far   12   120

11   barter fewest retrace targets adverse caterers extracts gag   24   132

12   Art Ada Aga Dax Dex Eve Eva Rex Red Eta Ted Wes Abe Asa Cec   12   144

13   Arab Bart Bess Brad Brit Fred Reed Sara Sade Tess Vera Bree   24   156

14   Gerda Steve Grace Texas Wertz Starr Besse Greta Edgar Freda   36   168

15   Baxter Carter Caesar Dexter Webster Stewart Barbara Rebecca   48   180

| 1 | 2 | 3 | 4 | 5 | 6 | 7 | 8 | 9 | 10 | 11 | 12

ALPHABETIC	19	ll dollar illegal fulfill allergy callous parallel bulletin	84
DOUBLES	20	mm jammed mammoth grammar immense dilemma commerce commands	96
(Continued)	21	nn winner manners connect planned dinners annually innocent	108
	22	oo poodle foolish schools flooded groomed boosting overlook	120
	23	pp puppet support clipper appeals hopping equipped happened	132
	24	rr arrive erratic borrows correct warrant currency arranged	144
	25	ss issues abscess process finesse success classify slowness	156
	26	tt better boycott attract matters attempt quitters bitterly	168
	27	zz sizzle fizzles buzzard dazzles puzzles blizzard embezzle	180
Fun Doubles	28	radii bazaar powwow flivver vacuum accommodation razzmatazz	12

71	**LONG**	29	unnecessary bookkeepers centennials recurrences inefficient	12
	DOUBLE-	30	necessarily innovations disseminate possibility predecessor	24
	LETTER	31	commissions corroborate annihilates accommodate allegations	36
	WORDS			

72	**DOUBLES**	32	Lynn Anne Bess Patty Leann Betty Wally Yvonne Debbie Noreen	12
	WITH	33	Ross Buzz Nell Bobby Eddie Kelli Gregg Doreen Miller Aileen	24
	CAPITALS			

73	**SPLIT**	34	big game│old doll│if found│the event│do orders│eager rascal	12
	DOUBLES	35	wet town│know who│maim men│will like│sit there│fourth house	24
		36	cold day│that the│off free│top prize│why yours│miss seasons	36

     │ 1 │ 2 │ 3 │ 4 │ 5 │ 6 │ 7 │ 8 │ 9 │ 10 │ 11 │ 12

91 FIRST FINGER	16	joy mun hum him noun Lynn phony mummy lymph humph hominy my	12
	17	you ohm inn Lyn hymn John union unpin ninny minim unholy Mo	24
	18	mum mon nun min hump July jumpy yummy nylon Yukon phylon Jo	36
92 SECOND FINGER	19	kin ink kink pink kiln mink link milky kinky pipkin minikin 12	48
93 THIRD FINGER	20	ill lop loom loll look only Polly jolly loony hilly million 12	60
	21	oil Lon lull polo poll pool Holly knoll Molly lolly mullion 24	72
94 FOURTH FINGER	22	pop pup pipy pump pomp puppy poppy plump nippy pupil pippin 12	84
95 MOSTLY RIGHT-HAND STROKES	23	bin dim bill book alloy annum chill alumni billion planking 12	96
	24	boy din bind boom amply apply chunk column humanly planning 24	108
	25	cup dip boil buoy annoy bloom dummy common joining platinum 36	120
	26	fly guy chin coin enjoy funny human comply jointly plumbing 12	132
	27	fun ham clip cook folio happy inlay employ killing pointing 24	144
	28	gum hay coil cool fully hello input injury milking replying 36	156
	29	hem key copy duly loyal minus penny junior nominal shipping 12	168
	30	hen pan cull dump mimic money phone lining plainly spelling 24	180
	31	jam pen doll film minor month photo lonely polices symphony 36	192

| 1 | 2 | 3 | 4 | 5 | 6 | 7 | 8 | 9 | 10 | 11 | 12

**DOUBLE-
LETTER
SENTENCES**

These sentences are
ideal for 1-minute
and 30-second "OK"
timings.

1 Bill will toss or miss the green fuzzy ball as it rolls by.   12
2 The dilemma expressed by the druggist annoyed all shoppers.   24
3 Puppeteers need good skills to make the puppets look funny.   36

4 Billie arrived to sweep the small floor with a green broom.   12   48
5 The bookkeeper withheld the inaccurately typewritten essay.   24   60
6 A million dollars was illegally appropriated by the robber.   36   72

7 Annie feels business suffers from excessive inefficiencies.   12   84
8 The shopper needs green cabbage and good apples for dinner.   24   96
9 He accepted suggestions between attempts to correct errors.   36   108

10 Rossi puzzles over excessive tariffs appearing on billings.   12   120
11 Debbie needs proof to withhold warrants from all employees.   24   132
12 Allergy sufferers seek all suggestions when summer sizzles.   36   144

13 Brigetta accurately adds bookkeeping to her list of assets.   12   156
14 Addie seeks proof that bigger bottles of apples are better.   24   168
15 Lorry agreed to vacuum the small attic and cook the dinner.   36   180

16 The beggar followed the dazzling flivver up the steep hill.   12   192
17 Bookkeepers need typewritten proof of any possible misdeed.   24   204
18 My sagging baggage suggests a bigger carriage is necessary.   36   216

Posttest

Repeat the 3-minute Pretest on page 39.

| 1 | 2 | 3 | 4 | 5 | 6 | 7 | 8 | 9 | 10 | 11 | 12

90 RIGHT-HAND WORDS

Keep both hands in the proper typing position.

When typing words with double letters accent the second letter of the doubles slightly.

1 ho in my no hum ilk mom nip lop ill oil mop pin you kin hip   12

2 on pi oh up ohm pip inn joy pup nun pop ink poi yum mon pun   24

3 hook kiln limp pomp nook oily puny link jump lily milk punk   12 36

4 loin hull pump moon null poll hymn loom upon pool honk lull   24 48

5 mull pulp only loll moll phon hypo look pony hill yolk pull   36 60

6 noun kilo holy pill hoop mill loop mump pipy kill loon hulk   48 72

7 hilly jolly kinky plunk mummy nippy puppy unpin imply humph   12 84

8 jumpy minim loony ninny polio yummy holly junky lolly pinky   24 96

9 poppy jupon humpy hooky plump knoll phony lumpy pulpy milky   36 108

10 hookup pippin homonym pinkily million nonunion polonium imp   12 120

11 lollop pompom minikin opinion minimum monopoly lollipop lip   24 132

12 Hun Joy Jon Kim Jim Kip Lum Kin Lil Lyn Lou Lon Min Loy Nik   12 144

13 John July Jill Lumm Lyon Milo Phil Lynn Lily Niki Ohio Polk   24 156

14 Hoppy Holly Jimmy Lilly Molly Polly Yukon Kinny Kippy Milly   36 168

15 Joplin Kokomo Philly Kimmon Johnny Phillip Milikin Hinkimin   48 180

| 1 | 2 | 3 | 4 | 5 | 6 | 7 | 8 | 9 | 10 | 11 | 12

DRILLS

75 COMMA KEY

Take a 1-minute timing on the Pretest. Practice the drill lines for 3 to 5 minutes. Then take the Posttest.

Pretest

1   When we attended that new class, we put in long, hard,   12
exhausting days. Indeed, the material was quite difficult,   24
and the room was hot. However, the kind, clever instructor   36
made it all worthwhile. In the evening, my friend, Debbie,   48
and I spent many hours reading, researching, and composing.   60

Practice

2 kkk k,k kkk k,k ,k, ,k, k,k kkk k,k ,,, k,k ,k, ,k, k,k ,,k   12
3 k,k k,k as, as, k,k is, is, k,k us, us, k,k to, to, do, do,   24

4 bank, link, rank, sink, wink, pink, junk, honk, dunk, bunk, 12 36
5 dads, port, dire, held, maps, care, zinc, half, page, papa, 24 48
6 both, wish, busy, duel, with, sign, very, firm, call, them, 36 60

7 however, recently, therefore, no doubt, of course, you see, 12 72
8 for example, obviously, consequently, in any case, perhaps, 24 84
9 at this time, for that reason, once in a while, frequently, 36 96

10 Of course, we will take apples, plums, oranges, and grapes. 12 12
11 Obviously, the excited, noisy kiddies will love these toys. 12 24
12 Look, we did that, Holly, but it was a long, long time ago. 12 36

Posttest

Repeat the Pretest.

| 1 | 2 | 3 | 4 | 5 | 6 | 7 | 8 | 9 | 10 | 11 | 12

DRILLS

Take two 1-minute timings on each drill. Compare the best timings on Drills 88 and 89. Practice daily for the slower hand (pages 49–54). If the rates differ slightly, practice equally for both hands. Take a Posttest in five days. Repeat if necessary to match the rates of both hands.

Pretest/ Posttest

87 ALTERNATE- HAND WORDS

1	cot own tub irk apt jam sue men die pan fit owl air hem and	12
2	they make town lend rich keys disk melt such isle chap hand	24
3	corn pane work lake city lend sock half also kept cork lame	36
4	girls amend blame formal bushel mangle eighty island profit	48
5	slept ivory their turkey height eighth handle social emblem	60

88 LEFT-HAND WORDS

6	are bag car dew fed gab rat saw tar vex war zag ace bar era	12
7	acre brag cafe data east fact gear rest scar tact vast west	24
8	zest beat crew deaf edge fret grew raft sear tart verb wart	36
9	areas brace ceded defeat estate facade garage rafter secret	48
10	taste verge wages averse beware crater debate egress fevers	60

89 RIGHT-HAND WORDS

11	hop ink kin lip mum nil ohm ply ump yip him imp lop mop joy	12
12	hulk inky join kink lump mink noun only pink upon yolk hump	24
13	junk kiln lion milk plum hunk jump pony link monk polo holy	36
14	imply lymph milky pippin pompon minion poplin unholy limply	48
15	nylon onion phony pinion kimono phylon pipkin uphill hominy	60

| 1 | 2 | 3 | 4 | 5 | 6 | 7 | 8 | 9 | 10 | 11 | 12

Pretest

1   Lt. Comdr. J. C. Greenburg served in the U.S. Army for   12
sixteen years. J.C. frequently was stationed in the U.S.A.   24
     He retired in St. Petersburg to prepare for his M.B.A.   36
as well as his C.P.A. J.C. graduated with academic honors.   48
     He joined the Acct. Dept. of the Edw. O. Long Mfg. Co.   60
J.C. got his C.P.A. before joining the U.S. Dept. of Labor.   72

Practice

2 lll l.l lll l.l .l. .l. l.l lll l.l ... l.l .l. .l. l.l ..l   12
3 l.l l.l dr. dr. l.l sr. sr. l.l fr. fr. l.l jr. jr. ea. ea.   24

4 coal. deal. dial. doll. foal. heal. foul. meal. oral. peel.   36
5 fair. dare. acre. cuff. acts. date. good. neat. case. hand. 12 48
6 much. hazy. even. rich. form. wish. bowl. upon. lady. hack. 24 60
7 odds. full. came. even. come. hash. barb. iron. data. inch. 36 72

Leave 2 spaces after a period at the end of a sentence.

8 Do it now. Go to town. See it soon. Handle it. The end. 12 12
9 Mail the card. See the boss. Do your job. Return it now. 12 24
10 Take your coats. Order the meal. Buy it. Run the errand. 12 36

11 Dr. F. R. Jones called Ms. Adams about the c.o.d. shipment. 12 12
12 F. B. Smith Mfg. Inc. ordered goods from the Wm. Thomas Co. 12 24
13 Maj. Gen. L. L. Howard earned his Ph.D. in Washington, D.C. 12 36

Posttest

Repeat the Pretest.

 | 1 | 2 | 3 | 4 | 5 | 6 | 7 | 8 | 9 | 10 | 11 | 12

83 PARENTHESES

20 lll lo9 l9l l(l l(l (l(l9l ;;; ;p0 ;0; ;); ;););) ;0; ;;;   12

21 in (a), (b), (c), or (d)|or (l), (2), (3), (4), (5), or (6)   24

22 call me (soon)|we meet (Friday)|I waited (for hours)|do (l)   36

23 The parentheses, (), are (l) easily used and (2) necessary.   12 48

84 QUESTION MARK

Leave two spaces after a ?.

24 ;;; ;/; ;;; ;/; ;?; ?;? ?;? ;/; ;;; ;?; ??? ;?; ?;? ?;? ??;   12

25 ?/? easy? unit? duly? kept? envy? your? cork? trout?   24

26 Why? Who? When? Who will go? Why did it burn? Why you?   36

27 Where shall we eat? At the Harbor Inn? At the Daly Manor?   12 48

85 THE DASH

28 ;;; ;p; ;p- ;-; ;-- ;-- ;-; --; --; ;;; ;-- ;-- --; --; ;;;   12

29 work--they| done--more| week--then| now--that| now--it| for--two   24

30 only--that| never--plan| time--not| spend--guests| more--favors   36

31 The painting--the one you wish to see--is in the next room.   12 48

86 PUNCTUATION SENTENCES

32 Why not send Lilly (the president) or Mack (the secretary)?   12 12

33 Send one--no, two--to get my order (at the new restaurant).   12 24

34 Will their trip be worthwhile (rewarding)--and inexpensive?   12 36

35 We've sent several (nine or ten); you send the rest--do it.   12 12

36 There's dinner (gourmet) in a flash--it's economical, also.   12 24

37 Tom asked, "Help me with my work?" "Doing what?" he asked.   12 36

| 1 | 2 | 3 | 4 | 5 | 6 | 7 | 8 | 9 | 10 | 11 | 12

1   The able-bodied, left-handed garage mechanic fixed the   12
worn-out equipment before re-marking the out-of-date forms.   24
His good-natured sister-in-law presented a scaled-down pro-   36
posal for a factory-installed, tuned-up engine. She should   48
receive unheard-of savings on an annual pay-as-you-go plan.   60
A straight-from-the-shoulder talk clarified this situation.   72

Practice

2   ;;; ;p; ;;; ;-; -;- -;- ;-; ;;; ;-; --- ;-; -;- -;- ;-; --;   12
3   ;-; ;-; up- up- ;-; to- to- ;-; it- it- ;-; be- be- or- or-   24

4   duty-free high-level short-term quick-freeze cross-examined   12 36
5   self-starters well-known black-tie self-control baby-sitter   24 48
6   sisters-in-law fathers-in-law editor-in-chief forget-me-not   36 60

7   well-read man two-hour debate one-cent stamp blue-gray coat   12 72
8   up-to-date letter first-class ticket high-powered runner-up   24 84

Return the carrier
after each hyphen.

9   for- one- blue- well- eight- child- narrow- formal- dismal-   12 12
10   now- tip- full- take- visit- turns- titled- height- profit-   12 24

11   Out-of-town guests put one-cent stamps on first-class mail.   12 12
12   My mother-in-law mailed a high-priced, up-to-date calendar.   12 24
13   The twenty-one-year-old man gave a much-talked-about party.   12 36

Posttest   Repeat the Pretest.

| 1 | 2 | 3 | 4 | 5 | 6 | 7 | 8 | 9 | 10 | 11 | 12

78 SEMICOLON

1 ;;; aaa ;;; aaa lad has; lad has; she led; she led; aaa ;;;   12

2 he called; we will; not yet; our text; to town; it will be;   24

3 for us; to go; and now; as yet; whenever; take care; truly;   36

4 Mary read; John spoke. It was lunchtime; no one was ready. 12 48

79 COLON

5 ;;; :;: ;;; ;;: :;: :;: ;;: ;;; ;;: ::: ;;: :;: :;: ;;: ::;   12

6 ;;; much: free: rail: mail: look: lake: fish: latch: 24

Line 7: Return carrier after each colon and double-space.

7 Dear Fred: Dear Sir: Ms. Jones: Dear Mary: Dear Carole: 36

8 Requirements: math and typing. Remember: Take them both. 12 48

80 APOSTROPHE

9 ;;; ;'; ;;; ;'; ';' ';' ;'; ;;; ;'; ''' ;'; ';' ';' ;'; '';   12

10 ;'; I'd I'd you'd you'd isn't isn't won't won't can't can't   24

11 cat's meow|we're told|shouldn't worry|can't see it|I'd call   36

12 My boss's chart listed a week's holiday. It's a good idea. 12 48

81 QUOTATION MARKS

13 ;;; ;"; ;;; ;"; ";" ";" ;"; ;;; ;"; """ ;"; ";" ";" ;"; "";   12

14 ;'; ;"; ;'; ;"; "Hello" "Hello" "Help" "Help" "Good" "Good"   24

15 "Good morning"|"Thank you"|"You're welcome"|"Take your car"   36

16 "Hal," he said, "we need a copy." "Certainly," he replied. 12 48

82 PUNCTU-ATION SENTENCES

17 Our boss's favorite remark was, "Make this one a rush job." 12 12

18 You said, "I'll mail it today"; however, it hasn't arrived. 12 24

19 The main idea is: Everyone should be involved; it's vital. 12 36

| 1 | 2 | 3 | 4 | 5 | 6 | 7 | 8 | 9 | 10 | 11 | 12